UNCOMMON MARRIAGE

UNCOMMON

learning about lasting love and overcoming life's obstacles together

MARRIAGE

TONY & LAUREN
DUNGY

WITH NATHAN WHITAKER

**TYNDALE™
MOMENTUM**

*An Imprint of
Tyndale House Publishers, Inc.*

Visit Tyndale online at www.tyndale.com.

Visit Tyndale Momentum online at www.tyndalemomentum.com.

TYNDALE is a registered trademark of Tyndale House Publishers, Inc. *Tyndale Momentum* and the Tyndale Momentum logo are trademarks of Tyndale House Publishers, Inc. Tyndale Momentum is an imprint of Tyndale House Publishers, Inc.

UnCommon is a trademark of Tyndale House Publishers, Inc.

Uncommon Marriage: Learning about Lasting Love and Overcoming Life's Obstacles Together

Designed by Dean H. Renninger

Edited by Kimberly Miller

Published in association with the literary agency of Legacy, LLC, Winter Park, Florida 32789.

Scripture quotations are taken from the *Holy Bible*, New Living Translation, copyright © 1996, 2004, 2007, 2013 by Tyndale House Foundation. Used by permission of Tyndale House Publishers, Inc., Carol Stream, Illinois 60188. All rights reserved.

Library of Congress Cataloging-in-Publication Data

Dungy, Tony.
   Uncommon marriage : learning about lasting love and overcoming life's obstacles together / Tony and Lauren Dungy, with Nathan Whitaker.
      pages cm
   ISBN 978-1-4143-8369-9 (hc)
1. Marriage—Religious aspects—Christianity. 2. Dungy, Tony. I. Title.
   BV835.D85 2014
   248.4—dc23   2013038252

Printed in the United States of America

20	19	18	17	16	15	14
7	6	5	4	3	2	

To our parents,
Doris and Leonard Harris
and
Cleo and Wilbur Dungy,
who modeled how to have
an uncommon marriage

Contents

Introduction

As we pulled into the school parking lot, I tried to let the moment sink in.

Our twelve-year-old son, Jordan, didn't pause to think about the significance of this day, however. As he glanced at his new school, nestled in a scenic woods setting, he was anxious for me to park so that we could walk back to the sixth grade pod and join the other students waiting on the back porch.

"Bye, Mom," he said before quickly giving me a kiss and taking off. As he disappeared around the corner, he yelled, "Love you!"

Jordan was ready for the start of sixth grade at Learning Gate Community School, itching to head inside for the latest adventure. He wasn't thinking about the doctors' prognosis that he might not live long enough to reach middle school. He wasn't counting the surgeries—more than thirty total—that he'd had since he was an infant. He wasn't fretting over the speech delay that still sometimes made finding just the right word difficult. Instead, he was eager to join the group of jumping and jostling classmates who were waiting for the bell to ring.

As Tony and I talked about Jordan's first day later on, we agreed that enrolling him in a mainstream classroom was an answer to twelve years of prayer. Who knew what more lay ahead for him?

Because of Tony's career in professional football, some aspects of our lives have been visible to the public. Yet it's largely the moments like this one—small but full of significance to us—that have defined our marriage. We believe it's because of our unwavering commitment to support each other and to live out certain principles that we have enjoyed a marriage spanning more than three decades—an uncommon feat in this day and age.

When Tony was coaching, we felt that one of our responsibilities was to model a strong and loving marriage to our players and staff. Now we feel ready to do that on a wider scale. That's not to say that we have it all figured out. We don't feel like experts, and the examples and principles we've tried to follow haven't resulted in a neat, tidy formula. In fact, we don't think that marriage can be captured through a formula or a "to do" list.

Relationships are challenging, especially because the miracle of two becoming one is such a mystery given each spouse's different personalities, desires, and passions. Some days, it seems like marriage is as much about hanging on for dear life, or just trying not to make things worse.

Before we tell our own story, we have to acknowledge that the longevity of our marriage is due, in no small part, to the examples our own parents gave us. Their examples were similar in important ways, like looking to the Bible for answers, but so different in the way those values were expressed in their daily lives. That has meant, at times, we have had to work through the different examples and resulting expectations that we brought into marriage.

So often in life and in marriage, we've discovered, there isn't a clear path. After all, as the apostle James wrote, "How do you know what your life will be like tomorrow?" (James 4:14). Instead, we walk forward, hand-in-hand, and *make* a path.

Looking back, we can see where we've come from and the ways in which the Lord has been present, even in those moments when we didn't know just *where* we were headed ourselves:

- when an anticipated career advancement didn't pan out
- when our expectations, formed as we were growing up in two very different families, clashed
- when I first moved hundreds of miles from my family
- when Tony's job demanded long workdays and extended stretches of time on the road
- when I felt blindsided by a major decision Tony made
- when our kids received extra scrutiny because of who their dad was
- when a middle-of-the night phone call plunged us unexpectedly into the fog of grief
- when we felt called to expand our family through adoption . . . many times.

We could go on and on. The point is this: we are convinced that there is power in story. We hope that something in *our* story will connect with something in yours.

Maybe you'll uncover a specific takeaway for you or your spouse. Maybe something we've experienced will be a warning to you—*I'd better not do* that! Maybe you'll better understand what happens when a biblical principle is lived out—or isn't. Maybe you'll simply experience renewed hope at the thought, *If* they *can make it work, so can we.*

Whether you are looking at the bleak remnants of a marriage that once seemed so promising, or at the fruit of a great marriage that has flourished, we hope the Lord will use this book to help and encourage you. If you feel that your marriage has hit rock bottom and you're not sure you can live another month, let alone another year, with your spouse, we strongly encourage you to get professional assistance as well. Some issues grow and fester over time, and you may need a pastor or other professional counselor to help you navigate them.

We have spoken with trusted friends and pastors numerous times in the past, both when life has been challenging and the going tough, as well as when times have been great and the wind at our back. In this book, we'll introduce you to a few of the couples who have mentored us along the way. Over the years, we've come to realize that working on our marriage relationship is always time well spent.

It is easy, as the late Stephen Covey pointed out, to let the urgent things of life crowd out the important things of life. There is a difference between the two. The good *can* be the enemy of the best. That is, there are wonderful opportunities in life, opportunities to do good with and for those around us. However, if we're not careful, those good opportunities can pile up and ultimately impinge on the truly critical priorities of our life.

Like our marriage.

We all must safeguard against that.

Tony's career has given us unique opportunities to be partners, both on and off the field. So when it came time to write this book, we quickly fell into a comfortable rhythm. We also made some interesting discoveries.

First, just because we have intentionally supported and encouraged each other doesn't mean we have agreed about every decision or always understood what the other was thinking. Loving each other doesn't mean becoming carbon copies.

Second, those differences, as perplexing as they can be at times, have actually made our marriage stronger and better balanced.

Third, some of our painful memories have been dulled with time. As we tried to recollect those difficult moments, we were pleasantly surprised to recognize that some of them which had been forgiven have truly been forgotten as well, swept away by the sands of time and the gentle breath of the Lord's forgiveness.

We entered into the writing process with the knowledge that a handful of things need to remain simply between us, as husband and wife. We trust you understand and hope that you won't even notice the few times we've exercised that right.

Writing this book has been a walk down memory lane for us, a chance to pause and reflect, even as life surges on around us, to remember many of the shared experiences of our thirty-plus years together. This journey has been more fun than we even anticipated.

More than anything, it has been a reminder that we have been blessed by a gracious, loving God who has walked alongside us every step of this journey, as well as by wonderful parents who blazed a trail for us.

We pray you will feel the Lord's presence in your relationship as well.

God Bless You,
Tony and Lauren Dungy

Chapter 1

BEGINNINGS

///////////////

Lauren

I couldn't figure out why my pastor, John Guest, kept trying to track me down. My mom told me that he had called three times in the past week. I hadn't missed church in quite some time, so I knew he couldn't be worried about that.

I didn't have the heart to tell my mom that our pastor had also stopped by the house once when she wasn't there—and I didn't answer the door. I'd been home alone when he drove up, and I was sure he was there to talk with my mom or dad. Not only that, but our church, St. Stephen's Episcopal, was quite large and proper. It just didn't seem right to me—answering the door for our senior pastor when I was dressed casually in shorts.

"Please call him back, Lauren," my mom said. "I'm sure it has something to do with the church and it must be urgent. Otherwise, he wouldn't keep calling."

It was a busy time for me—I had recently finished my second year of teaching sixth grade and now was engrossed in my own summer school classes. Still, I realized my mom was right. I needed to get back to him.

So I called the church office right then. John and I had a brief conversation in which he did most of the talking. When he finished, I remember saying, "I'll pray about it," before hanging up the phone.

Turning to face my mom, I said, "You'll never believe why he's been trying to reach me. He wants to introduce me to a *guy*—some football player with the Steelers. He's supposed to be a Christian, but you know I would never go out with an athlete." The truth is, I was seeing someone at the time—well occasionally, anyway. But when John mentioned the Steelers, I think I stopped listening. I had no desire to meet a football player or a coach. "I'll pray about it" was a polite way of saying "No, thank you."

While I enjoyed playing sports—I bowled, swam, and played tennis and other sports growing up—I had no interest in fawning over an athlete. My brothers were all athletic, and I had watched all the girls at school trying to impress them. They were great guys, but I don't know if those girls knew that. They seemed to be interested in them because of their status as athletes.

Not only that, but my primary focus in those days was my sixth-grade class at Edgeworth Elementary School. Teaching was the perfect career for me. I'd always loved working with children, developing young minds and helping them reach their potential. During junior high, my sister and I had even run an after-school program for neighborhood kids, helping them do crafts and other activities.

After earning my degree in elementary education from Duquesne University, I'd hoped to end up teaching seven- or eight-year-olds at an inner-city school similar to the one where I'd done my student teaching. God had other plans, however. When I graduated, I interviewed and was hired by the elementary school I'd attended, just down the street from my parents. I enjoyed being able to give back to Sewickley, a suburb northwest of Pittsburgh and the community that had given me so much growing up.

Though I'd expected to teach younger children, I loved sixth grade. My students were eager to learn and not yet struggling with so many of the issues that seem to crop up in middle school. Their parents valued education and were interested in and supportive of what was going on in my classroom.

At the end of each school day, I felt fortunate to be able to share the day's highlights with my own family. I was living at home with my parents; my siblings all lived in or near our family home too. Kevin, my oldest brother, was working and taking classes at the University of Pittsburgh. Averell, an executive with Equitable Gas, lived at home. My twin brother, Loren, was working as a store manager for Midas Muffler and living down the street. My younger sister, Taryn, was still doing her undergraduate work and attending Bates College in Maine. We were a tight-knit group.

My parents modeled very middle-class values. My dad, Leonard, was in real estate and was always looking at business opportunities. My mom, Doris, had stayed home for a while but then went back to work as a primary-care nurse practitioner. We kids knew our parents wanted us to work hard and help our household function smoothly. They expected us to do well in school and pitch in by doing chores and, when we were old enough, holding down part-time jobs. Finally, they expected us to graduate from college, as both of them had. It was a pretty simple formula for my parents.

My brothers were totally into football. Like them, I loved cheering for the "Black and Gold" every Sunday they played at Three Rivers Stadium. Unlike Kevin, Averell, and Loren, I never focused on any of the individual players. When John mentioned "Tony Dungy," that name didn't mean anything to me.

After finally learning why John had been calling and then promising him to pray about it, I tried to avoid him. I honestly wasn't interested in dating an athlete. His matchmaking didn't seem very promising, especially when John said he'd met Tony only once at a father-son breakfast at our church. Tony had been filling in for a Steelers player, Ted Petersen, who'd been the scheduled speaker but had to cancel at the last minute.

That's not to say I wasn't interested in meeting my future husband. My friends were getting married, and I looked forward to joining the married ranks myself. At the same time, I wasn't in too much of a hurry. I was going to wait on the Lord and make sure that it was His voice, not my own desires, that I was following. I was assured that He would answer my prayer in whatever timing He knew was best.

I didn't want to settle.

Plus, I was staying busy, which helped my patience. I certainly didn't anticipate that I would go off to college, return home, and find the answer at my church!

I may have had my doubts, but John wouldn't let it go; he kept telling me that Tony loved the Lord, and John thought we had a lot in common. He was so determined and convinced that God had ordained this relationship that he refused to give up until we had at least met once. I'm not sure I would have admitted it, but he'd piqued my interest enough that I eventually agreed to let him set up a time for me to meet Tony.

I was relieved when John suggested Tony come to my house, since I knew I'd have family around who could make excuses for me if I wasn't comfortable.

Tony arrived right on time that Friday morning. My dad had been coming down the hall when Tony arrived, and after greeting him, he began grilling Tony about the Steelers. My mom came out to meet Tony a few minutes later. Then my siblings began passing through as they were getting ready to go out for the day. By the time he'd been there about five minutes, Tony had met everyone. Tony says it was like a cartoon—one person would leave and another would show up—but he was simply seeing the normal bustle of our household.

I didn't say much at first, but I felt comfortable right away. Tony was smart and respectful, and he had gorgeous brown eyes. He was not at all how I'd pictured a professional football player and coach. He seemed like a nice person.

By the time the afternoon ended, I felt a bit sorry I'd put Pastor Guest off for so long. Then, just before he left, Tony told me, "Give me your number, and *maybe* I'll call you and we can play tennis sometime." I have to admit—I was a little put off by his attitude.

TONY

When I was saying good-bye to Lauren that day, she must have misheard me. What I actually told her was, "I'm headed to training camp and I'll be gone for the week, but if you wouldn't mind giving me your number, I *will* call you, and *maybe* we can play tennis sometime." She'd mentioned earlier that she enjoyed tennis, so I casually suggested we might do that when we got together next.

Lauren still disputes that, but I remember exactly what I said because I had been thinking about what I could say to leave her on the right note. I definitely wanted her to know I'd love to see her again and would call as soon as possible to set that up. When I drove away that afternoon, I thought things ended well, never suspecting she'd decided I must be one of those "players" who had a lot of girlfriends. Shows you the importance of communication in a relationship!

Except for that shaky ending, my experiences leading up to that first meeting were similar to Lauren's. When John first told me I had to meet a certain young woman from his church, I wasn't really interested. I'd only just met John the morning of the breakfast at his church. I had been looking for a girl like my mom—someone who was energetic, athletic, smart, and loved the Lord—and I wasn't against getting help in the search. Just not from someone I didn't even know. Not only that, but I was so quiet . . . what would I do if I didn't like this girl? Worse yet, what if she didn't like me?

By this point, I was only twenty-five, but my career playing in the NFL was already over. Back in 1978, I'd started my second year playing for the Steelers with high hopes, determined to make the transition from an obscure rookie to an established veteran. I led the team in interceptions that year—the same year we'd finished as the champions of Super Bowl XIII. Even so, I was just a backup player, not one of the stars. After that, I was traded to the 49ers and the Giants before finally being cut in 1980.

Suddenly my career in pro football had ended, and I was trying to find out what the Lord had in store for me next. That's when Coach Noll called and offered me a position on his coaching staff. So here I was, back in Pittsburgh. The morning of that breakfast, I never would have suspected that God might be using a pastor I'd just met to bring me face-to-face with my future wife.

I wouldn't have arranged to meet Lauren if John hadn't been so insistent. I couldn't help but wonder, *This is a church with five thousand people. There are no single guys she could get attached to in this church?* But while Lauren tried to avoid Pastor Guest, I tried to appease him. "Maybe you could just give me her number," I finally suggested. I figured that would get him to quit calling me and make all this go away.

"I'm sorry, Tony," he said, "but she's not the type who'd take kindly to you calling her directly, and she definitely won't call you. I really need to do it this way."

Finally, in mid-July, I agreed to meet her. The Steelers were opening training camp that week, so I told John I could see her the morning before camp opened. He pitched the idea that we meet at her house, and she said that would be okay.

When I got to the Harrises' front door, I took a deep breath and then rang the bell. I had no idea what to expect. When Lauren opened the door, I was *stunned*. She was far more beautiful than I could have imagined from John's description. She was slim and athletic with medium-length hair. She wore a sundress and little makeup. All of a sudden, the meeting that I had been pushing back from so hard seemed like a really good idea.

If I'd expected a quiet, awkward morning, I quickly learned that wouldn't happen. Lauren's dad, Leonard, greeted me, shaking my hand and welcoming me to their home. Lauren led me into the kitchen so we could talk. Her mom, Doris, came in a few minutes later to say hello. She looked as if she could have been Lauren's older sister. I got to meet several of Lauren's siblings, too, and I noticed that everyone in her family seemed to do everything at a high speed and high volume, often talking at the same time.

In that way, they couldn't be more different from my family. My parents, Wilbur and CleoMae Dungy, still lived in Jackson, Michigan, where I'd grown up with my brother and two sisters. My mom wasn't particularly quiet—she was engaging—but she was more reserved than the Harrises. And my dad was really quiet. He was a listener who would take things in, especially in new situations, and you would have to work extremely hard to draw things out of him. My mom probably contributed about 75 percent of the conversation in our home, whereas in Lauren's home it was the reverse: her dad was the talkative one. Beyond that, while Lauren's parents have always been expressive, my parents often have asked our opinion before weighing in on a subject.

I'd grown up in a stable, quiet household. My mom was from Canada and was teaching there when my dad started dating her. He was out of the Air Force and living in the Detroit area, traveling across the border to see her. They were both educators and thoughtful, and their four children were all good students.

My older sister, Sherrie, lived in Jackson, and our set of twins, Linden and Lauren, were in college on opposite sides of Michigan—Linden at Grand Valley State and Lauren at Oakland

University. We were pretty spread out. On the other hand, Lauren's living arrangement was fairly common in the Pittsburgh area. Most of the communities had very close families, where people often stayed close to home after they left high school.

Though our families might have been different in some ways, both my family and hers clearly loved, respected, and supported one another. That made me feel right at home, and I was fascinated by everyone's energy. The Harrises were so friendly that I didn't even mind when Lauren's dad and brothers asked me all kinds of questions about the Steelers.

As the morning wound down, I told Lauren that I'd be leaving for training camp soon but that Coach Noll always gave us Sundays off. That is when I got into trouble. To this day, I know without a doubt that I told Lauren I would call her and maybe we could play tennis. Now I realize that if a person doesn't talk loudly in the Harris home, he might not be understood, let alone heard.

Though Lauren was upset at what she saw as my arrogant attitude, she gave me her number, and I did call her that week from the hall phone in the dorm at camp. I picked Lauren up the following Saturday night, and we went to the Red Bull Inn, a chain restaurant near her home, for a quiet dinner. We talked and got to know each other a little, away from her family this time.

That was the start of a routine that continued into the fall. I would go straight to Lauren's house after practice on Saturdays. We usually played tennis, went bowling, or just hung out. I'd pick her up again on Sunday mornings for church. After that, we'd go out to lunch.

I found out later that since I'm naturally quiet and don't talk a lot about my feelings, Lauren wasn't sure during those first few months whether we were hanging out as friends—or as something more. I certainly thought we were dating. I was the first one off the practice field every Saturday, driving 85 mph on the Pennsylvania Turnpike to get to Sewickley and take her someplace. *Every* Saturday! To me, that was definitely dating, and I was loving it.

And to me, that was the perfect dating situation. Hanging out, having fun, talking with someone I liked. It was different than with any other girl I had ever met. It just felt natural.

We may not have openly discussed being serious or exclusive, but from the earliest days of our relationship, I was certain I had found my future wife. I knew I wanted her to meet my parents, so when they came to town for a game at the end of August, I took them to Lauren's house to meet her and her parents.

Considering how different our parents were, it's amazing how well they hit it off right from the start. They found plenty to discuss. Lauren's dad carried most of the conversation, but he and my dad talked a lot about sports and their time in the service during World War II. Our moms had a lot in common too. Both were proud of their families and talked about their children's accomplishments. Since my mom was a teacher and Lauren's was a nurse practitioner, they also swapped stories about their jobs in two different helping professions.

Lauren

Meeting Tony's parents was eye-opening in that his mom and dad were exact opposites from each other. His dad was very reserved—polite and more of a listener than a talker. His mom was bubbly and extremely outgoing. I could see the personality of a caring schoolteacher in her.

Though Tony's parents were extremely friendly, I couldn't tell if they liked me. Tony says he could tell they loved me from that first meeting, but they didn't share their feelings as readily as my family did, so I wasn't sure. But I definitely cared about how they felt about me.

That evening together confirmed what I'd begun to see: although Tony and I were raised with the same Christian guidelines, our family backgrounds were quite different. And that made our personalities and expectations—not to mention our childhood experiences—distinct.

For instance, I was surprised when Tony told me that, although his parents had always given him presents, he had never had a birthday party. When I was a young girl, birthdays meant celebrating with my family at Howard Johnson's over dinner and then digging into the complimentary slice of coconut birthday cake. We'd continue the celebration that weekend by inviting our friends and classmates to a festive themed party where we played games, ate lots of food, and had a wonderful time. So I couldn't believe that Tony had never experienced the fun of a birthday celebration. I decided right then to throw a surprise party for him.

For his twenty-sixth birthday in October, I invited some of his friends and former teammates, including the Shells and Stallworths, to my parents' home for a birthday celebration. The house was decked out with black and gold streamers and balloons. I'd planned the party around an Italian theme, so I served lasagna with Tony's favorite chocolate cake and ice cream.

That night Tony came in through my parents' kitchen door as he always did. He didn't suspect anything, so when everyone jumped up and yelled "Surprise!" he was totally shocked. He'd just left John Stallworth and Donnie Shell at practice, and now they were right here with the rest of us, waiting for him.

I think Tony appreciated the party, not only because it was his first one but because of the fun and laughter that night. When Tony saw how much joy it brought to me and everyone else to plan his party, it made an impact. He realized that celebrations—and not just for birthdays—were important to me and all the Harrises. In fact, every holiday was a major production when I was growing up. Our house was full of people celebrating and having a good time of fellowship.

Not only did I work to invite Tony into my world, I wanted to know more about his. I started reading the sports section of the *Pittsburgh Press* daily so that I could get a better understanding of what was going on in the football world. The Steelers were important to him, so I read the paper to make sure we could talk about what was going on in his life. I couldn't wait for Saturday to arrive so I could see Tony again. He was so down-to-earth and different from the other guys I spent time with.

Although we were spending a lot of free time together, as Tony mentioned, if somebody had asked if we were dating, I would have had to confess that I had no idea! About a month after his birthday party, Tony and I finally had the "talk." We were sitting in my parents' living room when Tony asked me where we stood—basically asking if we were exclusively seeing each other.

I asked, "Are we even dating?"

We finally got it straightened out that night. The answer to both questions was yes. We were dating, and we were exclusive.

I'm glad Tony was willing to broach the topic of our relationship when he did. One thing that attracted me to him was his consistency and steadfastness. Sometimes, though, he had difficulty showing emotion, which made it hard for me to know where we stood. As we edged toward marriage, I noticed Tony becoming more expressive. And he taught me an important lesson: not everyone finds it easy to reveal his or her deepest feelings.

Though I was more outgoing and social than Tony, even I was taken aback by the interest people had in professional athletes and coaches. Tony never appeared annoyed when we were interrupted by a fan, but I remember an early disagreement we had over this issue. We were at church when he got caught up in a conversation with someone who wanted to talk football. I was waiting for Tony in the parking lot by his car. The fan took advantage of the fact that Tony was too polite to walk away, and he kept talking. Eventually, I had to walk home because I couldn't find Tony.

I might not have been thrilled with the unexpected attention from sports fans, but by this point I had changed my mind about athletes. I realized I had been guilty of stereotyping them all as cocky and self-absorbed. Tony was so different from what I had imagined when John Guest first described him to me. I always knew that my knight in shining armor would be a stable, steady guy who loved the Lord; I never pictured anyone flashy. Tony fit every part of that role. I was quickly falling head over heels in love with him. He was definitely the type of guy whom I had dreamed about for so many years. I thought Tony and I were headed toward the altar, but he was still so guarded with his thoughts that I couldn't be sure.

TONY

John Guest had been right. He thought Lauren and I would hit it off, and we did. I like to think of it as divine intervention! She and I met in July but saw each other only on weekends until Labor Day. When training camp ended, we were able to spend much more time together.

Once I recognized that Lauren was the woman I'd been looking for, I knew I was on the path to marriage. So many people, especially today, live together before they're married, which seems like a mistake to me because the commitment isn't there. It takes commitment to make it through the tough times that come along when you're under the same roof with someone. Without the bond of marriage, it's too easy to just walk away.

As sure as I was that Lauren was the one I wanted to commit my life to, I have to admit that proposing to her was not my finest hour. The two of us were in her parents' family room when I began talking to her about the kind of woman I'd like to marry. I told her I was looking for a woman who loved the Lord, who wanted to use biblical principles to raise a family, and who was generous and caring. Lauren put on a good face, but she later told me that it wasn't at all clear to her at the time that I was talking about her. She thought I was asking for advice on how to find the right woman.

Of course, I had been describing Lauren as a way to lead into my proposal. After talking about the godly type of woman I was looking for, I told Lauren that she had all those qualities. Then I asked her to marry me.

Lauren said yes, despite my failure to be eloquent—or even to get down on one knee.

While I was still seated, I began fishing in my left front pocket for the ring I had bought her. Since I knew nothing about jewelry, I had gone to Don Duffy, a jeweler and the husband of one of Lauren's coworkers, and asked him to pick out a ring for me. Then I swore Don and his wife, Debbie, to secrecy until after I had asked Lauren.

We scheduled our wedding for summer 1982, eleven months after we met. During our engagement, we completed a premarital class through the church, which John required of any couple before he would marry them. Those sessions were extremely beneficial to us. Not only did we learn a lot about each other and the ways we would need to communicate, but the classes reinforced the fact that God's design was for marriage to be permanent. John emphasized that we would have to be totally committed to each other to make that happen.

Because our wedding would be in June, Lauren wouldn't have much time to finish wedding preparations after the school year ended, particularly since she loved her students and wouldn't shortchange them, even to plan her own wedding. But we knew if we pushed the ceremony back to July or August, we'd bump up against the Steelers' training camp and the beginning of a new school year. Lauren didn't want to return from her honeymoon and go right back to work or have me immediately head to training camp. She knew we needed some time as a married couple before resuming our busy work schedules.

Lauren

Thankfully, I didn't have to do all the preparation for the wedding myself. My mom acted as wedding planner and did a fabulous job. We enjoy a close mother-daughter relationship, so she knew me and my tastes. Together we planned a beautiful, intimate, Christ-centered ceremony.

My mom was so organized and meticulous that she handled the details and kept me updated on the progress while I finished the school year. I still remember her box of three-by-five index cards with the names and numbers of all the service providers and participants. She used tabs to divide the cards into sections related to some aspect of the day, such as the ceremony, the dress, or the caterer. I didn't have a wedding consultant, per se, but with my mom around, I didn't need one.

Tony and I agreed that we wanted an elegant wedding, but we didn't want it to become large and unwieldy. We quickly realized that between all the people I grew up with in Sewickley, all my coworkers from school, and all of the Steelers players, coaches, and staff, we were going to have a megawedding unless we had clear guidelines on whom to invite. But there was no way to do that without hurting people's feelings, so we limited the invitations to family only.

Since even our closest friends hadn't been invited, we didn't talk about the wedding much with other people. We knew they would wonder why they hadn't gotten an invitation. Still, our family and friends were excited about our big day and blessed me with several bridal showers. My mom and sister threw a shower for close family and friends. The parents of my sixth graders organized a surprise celebration, and the teachers at school threw a lovely shower for me as well. Tony even came to that shower, and I was so pleased that he had taken the time to stop by the school. I wasn't quite as thrilled that he showed up wearing his favorite shiny, brown-and-white checkered polyester shirt.

Oh, no, he didn't, I thought. *I just saw "the shirt" yesterday, and he is wearing it again today.* Tony loved that shirt because it was reversible—brown and white or white and brown. To him, that meant two shirts for the price of one. I may not have been crazy about the shirt, but I knew it was just a sign of Tony's practical side, and I loved having him there for the party.

Before we knew it, it was June 19, our wedding day. We were married at St. Stephen's, with John Guest officiating. My twin brother, Loren, proudly drove me up the street in his sparkling navy blue Chrysler New Yorker with its powder blue interior. He had hand washed and detailed every inch of the car to make sure it was perfect just for us. The service was at one o'clock. It was so beautiful and so meaningful—everything I always imagined my wedding would be. I cried tears of joy as we exchanged our vows and thanked the Lord again for answering my prayers.

Afterward, we had a reception in the church's lower level, which included a catered five-course meal. My mom wanted to be sure that Tony's family, who'd come in from out of town, were well fed!

Tony and I had a wonderful time at the ceremony and reception, and we looked forward to leaving on our honeymoon. Tony had told me that he had always dreamed of a romantic honeymoon in Hawaii, and he had suggested spending our wedding night at the Pittsburgh Hilton and flying to Honolulu the next day. I loved the idea of honeymooning in beautiful Hawaii, but the Steel City didn't strike me as a romantic starting point for our marriage. I had visions of getting married and boarding a flight that day. So we decided to spend the first two days of our honeymoon in San Francisco and then fly to Hawaii.

Once the reception was over, Loren drove us to the Pittsburgh airport. Earlier that day, my siblings had decorated his car with a "Just Married" sign and tin cans streaming from the back, just like in the movies. Talk about a different era—our entire family escorted us to the airport. We wouldn't have had it any other way!

Since security screening wasn't much of an issue back then, the Harrises and Dungys, still dressed in their wedding attire, waited at the gate to see us off on our flight. We were in high spirits when we boarded that plane. If we had known what a long day (and night) was ahead of us, we might not have been quite so lighthearted.

TONY

Thanks to careful planning by Lauren and her mom, the wedding had gone off without a hitch. When we left for San Francisco at five that afternoon, we had no reason to think the day wouldn't continue to run smoothly. After all, I'd made our hotel reservation and even arranged to borrow a car from Paul Hofer, one of my former 49er teammates.

The trip to San Francisco was a long one, since we hadn't been able to book a nonstop flight. Our plane finally touched down at about midnight. Paul and his wife met us at the airport and sent us on our way in their white convertible.

The first few minutes of the drive to our hotel were great. *How romantic,* I thought, *to cruise up the 101 Freeway in this sports car, the wind blowing through our hair.* But then Lauren told me she wasn't feeling well, so I stopped at a convenience store to pick up some medicine. Despite our weariness, the evening still might have turned out fine if I had not broken the car key off in the door. I called Paul from a pay phone, asking him to bring us a spare key.

We finally arrived at the hotel at 1:00 a.m., fifteen hours (with the time change) after our wedding ceremony had begun. When we stepped off the elevator on the eleventh floor, we looked at each other and smiled; we had survived the trip. Seconds later, the power in the hotel went out. With no light to see by, Lauren and I felt our way down the hallway until we found our room. But the truth of it is, with the lights out and nowhere to go, we were able to have the romantic evening we'd been looking forward to anyway!

Chapter 2

THE SKY'S THE LIMIT

///////////////////.

TONY

Just as our honeymoon hadn't started the way we'd expected, my first season as defensive backs coach turned out a bit differently than I'd anticipated, thanks to a players' strike.

Lauren and I didn't see that coming, though, when we returned from Hawaii. We were just glad to have several weeks to focus on each other before training camp and a new school year kicked off. I was grateful that Coach Noll insisted that his staff take off between the last minicamp in late spring and training camp in late July. He told us to make the most of that time—to get away from the game and concentrate on our home life—because he knew our focus had to be on football all season long. I was more than happy to focus on Lauren in the weeks just before and after our wedding!

In early August, I opened the paper to read an article affirming my instincts and potential as a professional coach. In fact, Chuck Noll said that my coaching future was unlimited, that "[Tony could] go as far as he wants."

Pretty heady stuff for me. My new, young wife seemed very impressed too.

Once training camp started, my routine was set. After spending all week at St. Vincent College in Latrobe, Pennsylvania, I would drive home on Saturday night, stay through church on Sunday, and then head back to camp. Occasionally Lauren would pack a picnic lunch and drive the fifty miles to camp to watch practice and then eat with me. She always brought my favorite foods—fried chicken, potato salad, and homemade chocolate chip cookies. However, she quickly learned that training camp was business time for the players and coaches.

The silver lining for us that year was the NFL players' strike. Seven games were canceled between late September and mid-November, so I was home much more that fall than I ever would be in the years to come.

That enabled us to make one change sooner than we might have otherwise. Now that we were living in Pittsburgh, we wanted to find a church there. Of course, since John Guest had introduced us, it felt a little awkward to thank him by leaving the church! At the same time, we knew we needed to find a church community that was closer to home and that fit us as a couple.

After we started praying about it, one of the Steelers' chapel speakers recommended Bethany Baptist Church. From the first time we visited, we loved Bethany, which was Bible-based, small and intimate, yet full of life. It was exactly what we were looking for.

Pastor Richard Allen Farmer and his wife, Rosemary, were special people. We met plenty of couples our age, but we also looked to some of the older ones to model marriage for us. We developed a close relationship with Mike and Barb Cephas, who had five children and were very active in the church. They welcomed us not only into the church but into their family as well. We became so close that we would later ask them to be the godparents of our children.

No one treated us like celebrities at Bethany. The families did a lot together—whether picnics or bike rides, potlucks or playing games—and while people were interested in discussing the Steelers, it was never the main focus of our conversations. That was refreshing for us. We weren't celebrities; we were just Tony and Lauren. An important part of our growth as a couple was being treated like any other people in the church.

If I had to name the number one thing that got our marriage off to a great start, it was finding the right church home. It provided a solid foundation for us as a newlywed couple. At Bethany, we established the habit of spending time talking about God—and to God—together.

Wednesday night was Bible study night, and Pastor Farmer would have us read different Scripture passages and pray in small groups. It was great for us to see so many couples, like the Cephases, praying together. Through their example, we learned how a marriage becomes stronger when couples make praying and spiritual conversations a priority. After all, spouses talk about everything else—why not their number one priority?

During our marriage, we've learned that how and when we connect spiritually may need to change. When we were first married, Lauren and I began praying together in the evenings after I'd come home from the office. Once our kids began arriving, we waited until we'd tucked them into bed. Now that I am no longer coaching, we find the best time for us to pray together is in the mornings. We make a point to get up fifteen to twenty minutes before the kids do so we can pray and read a devotion together.

Early on, we learned to ask God for two things when praying about decisions: first, that He would give us His infinite wisdom and direction, and second, that He would put us on the same page. Over the years, we've come to realize that when we are frustrated with each other, it's because we haven't spent enough time praying or communicating about spiritual matters to understand each other's heart on something.

Because of the players' strike, we were able to establish the practice of regularly praying together right away. Once the strike ended that November, however, Lauren was reminded what it meant to be a coach's wife when I would leave on Saturday morning for a road game. Weekends without her husband could be lonely.

Fortunately, she had company during my absences. Just before our wedding, I had decided to make the ultimate sacrifice and buy her a dog as a wedding gift. Growing up, Lauren's family had always had a German shepherd. Though I had never had a pet—not even a goldfish—I could tell while we were dating how much Lauren loved her family's dogs.

So even though I was not a dog lover and was even a little cautious around them, I decided to buy Lauren a German shepherd to show her how much I loved her. I asked her mom to help me but to keep it a surprise. Lauren's mom saw an ad in the paper for German shepherd puppies at a reasonable price, so I gave her the money and asked her to pick one out for me. The next time I came over to visit Lauren, her mom excused herself, drove over to pick up the puppy, and brought back the surprise.

Lauren was surprised all right. After gushing over the puppy and telling me how much she appreciated the gift, she said, "That puppy is so sweet and precious, but she doesn't look like a German shepherd." Her mom assured her she was, despite the dog's fluffy red coat. Lauren named her Casey because she looked more like an Irish setter than a German shepherd. In fact, after a few weeks had gone by, we still weren't sure what Casey was, but one thing was clear: our puppy was not a German shepherd.

I knew Lauren wanted a purebred shepherd, so I suggested we go to the breeders her family had always used so she could pick one out. She was ecstatic and selected a beautiful black and tan male puppy, which she named Corey. Now all along I assumed that once we got Corey, she would give Casey back. When I asked her about that, she said, "You let me fall in love with Casey, and now you want me to give her back? No way. I love that dog, red coat and all."

So now we had Casey and Corey, who got along great. But it didn't stop there. Lauren had been researching and reading about shepherds, and she said that if we were going to show and breed them, we needed both a purebred male and female. Months later we added Kippy, the female. My sacrificial wedding gift had wound up being *three* dogs.

Our stint in the dog show ring didn't last long. We competed with Corey until he outgrew his breed standards, and Lauren cared for the one litter that Kippy had. She didn't breed the dogs again, though, because she couldn't bear to see the puppies go to new homes when they reached eight weeks.

We did agree on some ground rules for our dogs. For instance, Lauren assured me she would not let them in the bedroom. That's why I was sometimes surprised when I called her from training camp or a road game at night.

"What is that breathing in the background?" I would ask. "The dogs aren't in the bedroom, are they?"

Lauren

While Tony was traveling with the team that first year, I used to have both Casey and Corey in bed with me. When he called at night and asked me if they were on the bed with me, I didn't deny it. I told him, "It was just so quiet, and I thought I heard something." My parents' home had always been filled with talking and laughter; now I was alone in a home near woods that felt pretty remote. Also, I knew if anyone was paying attention to the Steelers' schedule, they'd know that Tony was out of town and that I was home alone.

I also remembered what Paulette Shell had told me. The year Tony played for the 49ers, she and her husband, Donnie, who was still playing for the Steelers, rented Tony's house. Paulette told me she was always afraid when her husband was gone. She'd hear noises and put chairs against the doors to feel more secure. I used to tease her because the neighborhood seemed so quiet, friendly, and safe when Tony and I were dating. But that was because Tony was always there with me. When he went away to camp that first night, I started hearing strange sounds too. But I had my loyal and faithful dogs to keep me company and protect me.

During the early months of our marriage, I began redecorating Tony's bachelor pad, remaking it into our family home.

His three-bedroom brick house was charming and spacious but needed a woman's touch to bring out its potential. In the living room, he'd stacked the television and lamps on cardboard boxes. I replaced them with end tables. And the colors in the house were dark and masculine, so my mom and I made the rooms brighter and cheerier and arranged everything so our home fit us as a couple.

Tony told me that he appreciated having a woman's touch around. Changing the decor was just one of many transitions after getting married; we had a lot to learn about each other since we'd met only a little over a year before. We wanted to spend good quality time together, growing in our relationship with the Lord as we grew closer to each other.

We knew we didn't want to start a family right away. Our differences reminded us why it was important that we get to know each other as husband and wife. Not only that, I was still teaching and wanted to continue developing my career. I enjoyed my students so much that I wasn't focused on having children of our own yet.

Tony and I had many opportunities to nurture kids as a couple, too, because Bethany embraced the concept that every child should be cared for by the church. Bethany had programs that reached out to the community, such as vacation Bible school and after-school tutoring and activity programs for young people. I was involved in the Sunday school program, and on top of that, many of our friends at church had children. So whether we were going to their houses or they were coming over to see us, we were always around children. Sometimes we'd even invite kids to spend a weekend with us so their parents could get away. We knew we would have kids of our own eventually, but at that point, with Tony coaching and me teaching, we were happy just to be a support system.

A couple of years into our marriage, though, God made it clear that He had other ideas for us regarding children. During one Sunday service, a group appealed for help from the congregation, telling us about the shortage of willing foster parents in Allegheny County.

Tony and I decided to meet with the guest speakers after the service. They'd set up a little table in the back of the church where they handed out information and answered questions. We also watched a video about foster parenting. We left feeling that we could give children some of the love and attention they weren't getting in large group homes.

We continued to pray about it and decided to investigate a little more. We had to have a home study and some background checks done, but soon after that we were approved to be foster parents.

It was such a natural thing for us to do. I guess in the back of my mind I remembered my parents hosting foreign exchange students or caring for kids from group homes in the Pittsburgh area who came to our home for a weekend. Later my mom and dad became foster parents and opened their home to over seventy children. In the early nineties, they would end up adopting two of them, Amanda and Devin, bringing the total number of my siblings to six.

On top of that, many young couples in our church were already foster parents. Because of the mutual support and encouragement Tony and I found at Bethany, we were both on board with the idea.

We completed the training program on a Friday, and that

same night we received our first call. The social worker asked if we would be able to take in a little boy named Gypsy. He turned out to be an adorable little seven-year-old boy with curly black hair. He arrived with just the clothes on his back and an infectious smile on his face.

Although he was well behaved and extremely intelligent, early on I thought he might have a tendency to make up stories. For example, it bothered me when he told Tony and me about his eight brothers and sisters, whom he said were "living in California in a shelter with the nuns." When I expressed my concerns to his social worker, she said, "He *does* have eight siblings, and they *do* live in California." Apparently, he had been separated from them at the shelter and was sent back to Pittsburgh to live with his mother.

We ended up caring for Gypsy for over a year. His sweet sister Jayme was in our home for a number of months too. Several times the social worker informed us that a court date for a custody hearing had been scheduled. As the date rolled around, Gypsy would say, "My mom's not gonna come. She's too busy doing other things." Each time the social worker picked him up, though, we'd say a tearful good-bye, thinking we wouldn't see him again.

Gypsy was always right; his mom wouldn't keep her appointment at the hearing, and he would be back with us that evening.

This little boy was used to being bounced around. It was troubling. After one court date, though, we didn't hear a word until late that night. I told Tony sadly, "Well, that's it. He's not coming back." As we were going to bed at about ten, the doorbell rang. By the time we got to the front door, Gypsy had his little button nose pressed up against the window, and when we opened the door he kept saying, "What took you so long to answer the door?"

I had never imagined it would be Gypsy. As he walked in, he asked matter-of-factly, "Mom Lauren, what did you make for dinner? I'm starving."

If the uncertainty was hard on us, it was excruciating for Gypsy. On the one hand, he just wanted to be reunited with his siblings. He wanted his family to be together. On the other hand, he liked the stable environment in our home. He appreciated having a predictable schedule and knowing what was going on every day. He loved the security of knowing we would be there when he woke up in the morning and when he went to bed at night.

One of Tony's former teammates, Jon Kolb, owned a farm where he kept quite a few animals, including horses. Gypsy loved the peaceful and tranquil environment when we took him there one Saturday, so we went a few more times. During our visits, Gypsy purposely began leaving things behind, like a toy or piece of clothing. He'd had so many disappointments and broken promises that he didn't believe us when we told him we could come back again. If he left something, he figured we'd have to go back and get it.

We finally had to let Gypsy go because the social worker wanted to reunite all nine siblings in one home. We felt that we were too young and that it was too early in our marriage to take on nine children. And that broke my heart. I remember crying for several days when Gypsy left.

The toughest part of fostering, in fact, was never knowing how long we were going to have a child with us. Sometimes we had a boy or girl overnight; other times, a child would stay with us until the parent's next court visit.

We did sense that the Lord wanted us to help by being foster parents, but it was tough developing an emotional attachment and then watching the kids leave, never knowing what happened to them after they left our home. The rest of fostering was easy: there was a crisis situation and a child was in danger. The social workers needed to place them in a safe home, not a police station or an office building. Those children needed stability, and we could provide the room—it was that simple.

TONY

As God was bringing foster children into our lives and preparing us for our own children one day, He was also helping us learn to adjust to the differences in the families we'd grown up in. Because we lived in Pittsburgh, we spent more time with Lauren's family. I enjoyed being around my brothers-in-law, even though it was not at all like being with my own sisters and brother. While my family had opinions, they usually waited until someone asked what they thought before speaking up. Lauren's brothers didn't hesitate to ask personal questions, and nothing was off limits. When we'd make a major purchase—like a house or a car—they'd ask, "Where did you get it?" "How much did you pay?" and "What were you thinking?"

Their questions weren't limited to our home life either. As soon as Lauren's brothers walked through our door, they'd start telling me what defense the Steelers should run the next week or what had gone wrong the week before. While their probing caught me off guard at first, I quickly realized it was their way of showing that they cared about me and that they welcomed me into the family as a brother. They wanted me to be successful, and analyzing and scrutinizing everything I did was their way of helping. Also, I knew the Bible said, "There is safety in having many advisers" (Proverbs 11:14), so I was open to their advice.

While I adjusted to getting her brothers' input about everything, Lauren learned to accept my parents' unpredictability whenever they came to visit. The Harris home had been more structured than mine, with a fairly regular schedule and dinner hour. Early in our marriage, my mom and dad often drove from Michigan to attend Steelers games, but they didn't always let us know what time they would arrive. Sometimes they even stopped by the mall before coming to our home.

Lauren felt she should serve my parents a proper meal and make them feel welcome, but that could be difficult because she was never sure what time they'd arrive. Sometimes, when it was approaching ten or eleven at night and we still hadn't seen them, Lauren even worried that they'd run into trouble on the road. Rather than stay silent, Lauren eventually told them her concerns. When she did, my parents reassured her that they didn't mind eating late and promised to let her know if they were delayed on the road so she wouldn't worry about their safety.

I admired Lauren's willingness to speak up when necessary, and she sometimes encouraged me to do so as well. For example, when Woody Widenhofer, the Steelers' defensive coordinator, left to become head coach of the USFL's Oklahoma Outlaws, I thought I was in line for his job. Coach Noll had never talked to me about it, but he wasn't interviewing other coaches either.

Lauren kept telling me, "If you want the job, go in and discuss it with Chuck." But I've always felt that if you have to come out and ask, you're not going to get the position.

A couple of weeks after Woody left, Chuck and I were in New Orleans for the Scouting Combine, an opportunity for

NFL scouts to watch guys who will be in that year's draft work out together. One evening Chuck asked me if I wanted to take a walk with him to Preservation Hall. I agreed, and I was sure he would use that occasion to tell me I was going to get the job, but he really did just want to go listen to jazz, one of his passions. He said nothing at all about the defensive coordinator position.

I went back to the hotel and called Lauren. She asked, "Well, do you have the job?"

"I don't know!" I said.

Lauren was shocked. "What did you two talk about? How did you end the conversation?" She finally convinced me to at least talk with Coach Noll to find out if he was going to promote me or if he'd decided to go in a different direction. He looked surprised when I finally got up the nerve to ask him about the opening.

"Of course I'm promoting you," he told me. "You know more about the defense than anyone else on the staff." Apparently his decision was so obvious that he hadn't even mentioned it.

Along with the new responsibility, I got a raise, which enabled Lauren and me to look for a new house. We both liked where we lived, but in the back of Lauren's mind, she wanted to select a home together, as husband and wife. Because her dad was a real estate and insurance broker, he often told us about new developments and offered to show us new listings—all of which coincidentally happened to be closer to the Harris family.

We finally settled on a four-bedroom colonial home in the North Hills area of Pittsburgh, not far from Lauren's family. John Kolb loaned us his flatbed truck from the farm, and it seemed as if everybody from Bethany turned out to help us pack and load the flatbed. It was like a big church-wide event, with friends loading up our belongings and driving with us to our new home.

I'm not sure what the neighbors thought. Rather than watching uniformed workers and professional moving vans, they saw forty people and a big flatbed truck. We looked like the Beverly Hillbillies as we drove up the street with our possessions secured with ropes to the truck, but it was another great Bethany moment. And when we finished the job, Lauren spread tablecloths on our lawn to set up a lunch and feed the famished workers.

Lauren

With two acres of property, we had plenty of room to entertain guests in our yard. We also had room for a vegetable garden. As I was planning out the garden shortly after we'd moved in, I had my first long, in-depth conversation with Tony's dad, who was visiting from Michigan.

I had taken him out to the garden and asked him how many inches apart I should plant the green beans. Two hours later, he was still telling me about soil content and photosynthesis. I was burning up in that hot July sun but I loved spending time with him and hearing his knowledge and wisdom. That was the day I discovered that Wilbur Dungy was indeed a man of few words—until you asked him about something he was passionate about. He was a biology teacher with a world of knowledge about the outdoors and plant life specifically.

Now that Tony and I had a couple of acres of rolling hills, we bought a riding mower. I'd always wanted to mow the grass when I was growing up, but that chore was delegated to my brothers while my sister and I were responsible for the laundry and indoor cleaning. I didn't mind our defined roles and the order and structure they brought, but at times I would have enjoyed doing some of those things my brothers did. When neighbors would ask Tony or me why he made me cut the grass, I told them he wasn't forcing me. I loved being outdoors, along with the instant gratification that comes from a nice-looking lawn and the smell of freshly cut grass.

After Tony's promotion and our move into a new home, I left my teaching position to be at home full time. We now felt ready to start a family. Beautiful Tiara Nicole was born in late 1984. She looked like a baby doll with her delicate features and angelic face. I would hold her for hours and marvel at how beautiful she was. Having a new baby in the family is a huge transition for most couples, but it really wasn't for Tony and me. My mom stayed with us for the first few weeks to help out, and I was grateful for her support. But we had so much child-care experience and preparation from teaching and caring for foster children and babies at church that Tiara's arrival didn't seem to change much of anything. She was the ideal baby, sleeping through the night in no time.

God's timing seemed perfect, since once we were in the new house, our support system was that much closer to us. My parents and aunts and uncles in the Sewickley area were eager and available to help with Tiara and anything else we needed. And within minutes of walking through the church doors, someone was taking Tiara in her arms to hold and cuddle.

Handsome James Anthony, whom we lovingly called Jamie, was born just over two years later. At nine pounds and twenty-one and a half inches long, he seemed destined to be the next Magic Johnson. When he was born, the spoiling from family started all over again! Tony wasn't sure Jamie would get quite as much attention since he was a boy, but that wasn't the case. Both babies spent many weekends at the home of my parents, whom the kids called Grandma Bird and Pop Pop. They always came home with new outfits and toys and were worn out from all the love and attention doled out to them.

By the time Jamie was born, Tony and I had been married just over five years. We didn't think life could have been much better. To start our family life in my hometown of Pittsburgh, where Tony was able to work for Chuck Noll, was such a blessing.

It was a great time in our lives, but a time that would not last forever.

Chapter 3
HAIL TO THE CHIEFS

Lauren

The cold January morning started off like so many others. I bundled up Tiara and Jamie in matching red snowsuits and headed over to the Northside Library for story time. As a former teacher, I loved the opportunity to introduce them to good books; as a stay-at-home mom, I relished the chance to get out and mingle with other young moms.

Just before the librarian asked us to sit down so she could start the story, Tony rushed in, looking for me. He caught me off guard. My first thought was, *Oh, he came to surprise the kids and join us for story time. How sweet!* But I could tell by the expression on his face that something was troubling him. Pulling me aside, he quietly told me about a disturbing request Coach Noll had just made of him. Chuck had asked him to step down as defensive coordinator and resume his former position coaching the defensive backs. I had barely taken that in when Tony mentioned that he was thinking of looking for a job with another team.

I was stunned and didn't know what to think. Was Tony actually talking about leaving the Steelers? Just like that? How quickly our idyllic world was being turned upside down. I had always assumed we'd be working for the Steelers forever. Most of the coaches on the staff had been there for over fifteen years, and we had never entertained the thought of moving.

I was close to many of the wives of Steelers players, including Paulette Shell, Flo Stallworth, Maxine Willis, and Le'Chelle Johnson. We had developed friendships that went beyond the X's and O's of football and had enjoyed so many fun times. Our children went to birthday parties, playdates, and community events together. We watched one another's kids when one of us had to travel out of town. So I certainly wasn't anxious to leave my friends, not to mention my family. I guess that in the back of my mind I always knew Tony might leave to coach another team. But I had assumed that it would be due to a promotion and that such a move would be sometime in the distant future.

This was the first time I personally experienced the tough side of the NFL. I had seen other families experience it. Whenever players whose wives I had been close with had been cut or traded, I always felt bad. I would stay in touch with them and try to help them deal with the sudden changes in their lives. Now it was happening to us, to my family! It was painful, even though Tony pointed out that this might be the Lord's way of moving us along. That didn't make it any easier. And, by the way, where was He moving us? We had no idea.

I was crying and very emotional, but I told Tony I would support him either way. If he wanted to look for another job, I didn't mind moving. That was the sacrifice you made for life in football. I was in it with him.

TONY

I was pretty shocked by Chuck Noll's request in early 1989 as well. After drafting a promising defensive class in 1987, the Steelers seemed poised to play even stronger the following year. But then two of our best players, Donnie Shell and John Stallworth, retired, and Mike Merriweather, one of our defensive leaders, missed the entire season due to a contract dispute. As a result, we went 5–11 in 1988, missing the playoffs for the fourth straight year. Feeling the heat, Coach Noll asked me to step down as coordinator but remain as the defensive backs coach.

I knew Lauren was at the Northside Library with the kids that morning, so after leaving Coach Noll's office, I left the stadium and went to find her. Like Lauren, I had not given any thought to leaving Pittsburgh. When we had celebrated our sixth anniversary the previous June, Lauren and I had reflected on our many blessings. Our kids were thriving, and we had built some strong relationships at our church. Lauren and I were also growing together through a Steelers Bible study that met weekly for spiritual growth and fellowship.

But if I stayed with the team, I would have to take a demotion. Neither Lauren nor I felt that was fair, nor would it be in the best interest of my career. If I decided to resign, though, I had no idea where we would go. How would I even look for another job in the NFL? Who knew where we would end up?

The unknown was intimidating to both of us. We wanted to stay in Pittsburgh, but as we prayed about the situation, it became clear the Lord was closing that door.

While it was uncomfortable, I was close enough with Coach Noll that I was able to be candid and tell him that I would rather resign than accept a demotion, so I started looking for another job right away.

I made a lot of calls and talked to a lot of people in the NFL during my job search. In the end, we had four viable options: Cincinnati, Kansas City, the New York Giants, and San Francisco. My first choice was to go to Cincinnati, in large part because of the Bengals' head coach, Sam Wyche, who was an assistant with the 49ers when I played for them. Not only that, but Cincinnati was close to Pittsburgh and seemed like a similar city. Plus, the Bengals had good teams and were playing in the Super Bowl that year.

Sam called me from Miami, where his Bengals were preparing to play the San Francisco 49ers in the Super Bowl. He told me his defensive line coach was leaving after the game, and he wanted to hire me if I was interested. But after the Bengals returned home, Sam called me with bad news. Mike Brown, the team's owner, was concerned I wouldn't be content in the defensive line coach's position for long and might not stay in Cincinnati. Unfortunately, Sam told me, he was going to have to hire someone else.

God had closed one door, but three others were still open. Lauren and I simply had to figure out which to go through. Shortly after my final conversation with Sam, Bill Walsh, head coach of the Super Bowl champions, the San Francisco 49ers, called. He told me that he was retiring and that George Seifert was taking over as head coach. One of Bill's other coaches, Denny Green, had just taken the Stanford head coaching job, and the team wanted me to coach the 49ers' running backs. I knew Bill, George, and the other coaches out there, also. I had a lot of respect for those men, and the team had some great players!

It would have been a good career move. They wanted me to coach offense, which would have broadened my horizons professionally. Yet the team's location, a big city on the West Coast, didn't seem right to me because of where we were as a young family.

I also flew to New York to talk with the Giants' Bill Parcells, another coach who had led his team to a Super Bowl championship. Bill was putting together an excellent staff and team. My interview went well, and I knew I would grow professionally there as well. But New York? Lauren and I were nervous about that too.

Lauren

Tony's job search was a little nerve-racking for me at first. Every time the phone rang, I wondered whether this was the call that would impact our family's future. Tony kept me abreast of everyone he was talking to, and we discussed the pros and cons of every situation. And we prayed—a lot! I appreciated that Tony wasn't just looking at the teams. He was looking to make a good move for us as a family.

Like Tony, early on I was sure we'd be moving to Cincinnati. The position seemed so right to us. Tony knew the head coach and was excited about the opportunity there. The city was only a couple of hours from Pittsburgh, so the move wouldn't be that big of an adjustment for me. Cincinnati was even closer to Tony's parents, so the kids would get to spend more time with his side of the family.

As we watched the Super Bowl on television, I almost felt as if we were at the game. I found myself getting excited, rooting for Cincinnati. That was a strange feeling because they were the Steelers' big rivals. I would have never cheered for the Bengals in the past. But now, there I was, yelling and screaming for them because we thought this would be our next place of employment. I was thinking of the Bengals as *our* team!

But Tony and I have found that what seems so perfect to us isn't always what God has in mind. That was the case this time. God closed that door in Cincinnati, so we had to encourage each other with the reminder that He was in control of our situation.

I was grateful that Tony had several other opportunities to consider. I wasn't surprised when Bill Walsh called. But San Francisco seemed so far away. I didn't know much about the city; however, Tony always told me how happy he was to get back to Pittsburgh after playing out there. It was a much bigger city, and our kids were so young! I knew the team had just won the Super Bowl, so joining them would have been great for Tony's career. I wasn't sure, though, how good such a move would be for the rest of our family.

New York concerned me for similar reasons. When Tony told me how much the houses cost in New Jersey and how far we'd have to live from the offices to make it work, I grew more and more uncomfortable about living there.

We joke a lot about getting so much advice from our families on major decisions. But even when we were dating, I could see that Tony was seeking input from wise counselors. After we were married, I knew we'd make the final decision on things ourselves, but we always welcomed input. When we bought our house in Pittsburgh, my family was there to help us and, as always, everybody weighed in. Tony told me he was fine with that. He knew they were giving advice not because they didn't have confidence in him but because they loved me and wanted to help.

As we considered this move, though, we didn't seek a lot of input from our family and friends. Many people offered Tony advice on what he should do. But to us, this was as much a family decision as a football decision. We knew that other people didn't necessarily understand what was most important to us. We desired peace of mind for ourselves.

Prayer was extremely important, and we talked with some of our close Christian friends. But more than anything, we talked to each other.

TONY

Just a couple of months before we left Pittsburgh, Pastor Farmer preached about knowing when the time was right for the Lord to bring something new in your life. He said that when God was moving in that way, you couldn't stand pat, even if it felt more comfortable. And then he dropped a bombshell on the congregation: he was leaving Bethany to be a dean at Gordon College outside of Boston.

Little did Lauren and I know on that Sunday that we would be calling Richard just a few weeks later to talk over that same question in our own lives. His message was powerful and continued to resonate with us once we began trying to discern where God was leading us.

And then Marty Schottenheimer offered me a job in Kansas City coaching the defensive backs. Marty had just left the Cleveland Browns in a dispute with the owner over assistant coaches. I was hoping he would hire me as his defensive coordinator, but that position was going to Bill Cowher. Bill had worked with Marty in Cleveland, and Marty told me he couldn't promote someone from the outside over coaches who had been with him. That seemed fair to me. In fact, I appreciated his loyalty to staff members.

Lauren and I continued to talk and pray about this move, even as all three coaches began pressing me for a decision. There was no booming voice from the sky clearly telling me which way to go. Both the Giants and 49ers were Super Bowl–caliber teams, while Kansas City was coming off a losing season. In the end, however, I didn't feel comfortable taking my family to either of the two big cities. So after being disappointed about not being able to go to Cincinnati, Lauren and I decided Kansas City would be the best place for us. Tiara and Jamie were so young at the time—four and two—it just seemed like the best fit.

Still, we were about to leave our comfort zone in Pittsburgh. We knew everybody there, and we knew our routine. Kansas City was going to be completely new. At the same time, it was exciting. Just us, blazing a new trail.

After accepting my new job as the Chiefs' defensive backs coach, I went out to Kansas City right away. Not only would I start working but I wanted to find my way around and try to begin to get us settled. Meanwhile, Lauren stayed behind in Pittsburgh, preparing to get our home on the market.

This was my first job change as a married man. It was also my first time coaching outside the Steelers' organization. I quickly found out that some things would be different, starting with the working hours. They were much longer under Marty than they had been with Chuck, and that would take some getting used to. While Lauren and I weren't thrilled to be apart, it was just as well that she, Tiara, and Jamie were able to enjoy their last few months with family and friends in Pittsburgh while I adjusted to a much longer workday.

I rented an apartment with Bruce Arians, another coach who was new to the Chiefs' staff. For four months, we were engrossed in our new jobs, trying to get acclimated and meet our new players. But we missed our families tremendously.

Lauren

The NFL doesn't have a relocation program, so the wives usually take care of everything prior to a move. I met with realtors and then followed their suggestions on what to do to get the house ready to be shown. I was advised to have a lot of small repairs and painting done to make the house appealing to prospective buyers. Once our home was on the market, it was a daily challenge to keep the house spotless with our two young, active kids and all their toys. So while we weren't thrilled to be apart, I had enough to do to keep me busy in Tony's absence.

Even so, I felt some anxiety. Tony had moved several times as a player, but this was uncharted territory for me. I'd never lived outside of Pittsburgh or more than twenty-five minutes away from family. Kansas City—while closer to my hometown than San Francisco—could have been on the other side of the world as far as we were concerned. We didn't know anything about the city, nor did we have any ties there, so this was really a step of faith. When we decided to go, it certainly felt like we were severing ties with our Pittsburgh family, our church, and our friends.

I knew my family would still reach out to us and support us from a distance, but it wouldn't be the same. Tony and I would have to make more of the big decisions on our own. As frightening as that was, in the back of my mind I thought, *Maybe that will be good for us.*

I remember flying out to Kansas City to go house shopping. Tony and I looked at dozens of homes, some in Kansas and some in Missouri. So many different choices made the search exciting, but everything was so new. How would we decide whether to live in Kansas or Missouri? In this subdivision or that one? Should we go with a ranch-style home or a two-story?

My family was still eager to hear about our options, so we would tell them about some of the homes' features. As strange as it seems now with the availability of cell phones, we had to mail pictures to them and wait a couple of days for their response. Still, we knew they couldn't examine everything first-hand and help us out as they had in the past. We would have to make some major decisions on our own.

That's when we relied on our faith too. We had to actively pray about our decisions. In the past it had been easy to say, "Well, I'll pray about it," all the while knowing we could pick up the phone and call family members for their advice or to ask them to check something out. In Kansas City, we really had to trust the Lord and lean on Him for advice and guidance. That definitely made it a growing experience for us.

We ended up buying a house in Overland Park, Kansas. "Kansas?" my Pittsburgh friends would say. "Will you get to meet Dorothy?"

Although many of the houses in the area were older and stately, we bought our home, which had an open and airy contemporary plan, in a new subdivision. The large kitchen, or "hearth room," had a fireplace and was a primary gathering area, which was so different from our house in Pittsburgh. Each bedroom had its own bathroom, and we had a three-car garage. We got a house with all these features for about what we'd paid in Pittsburgh for the house we'd just sold.

At last, the kids and I would be able to join Tony for good. As our furniture and other belongings were packed on the moving van, I realized that I'd never known how much we'd accumulated until we had to move it!

My family took us to the airport. I carried a number of items I hadn't wanted to risk being damaged on the moving van. In addition, I was weighed down with toys and books to keep the kids occupied on the plane.

Then there were our three dogs—Casey, Corey, and Kippy. They were kenneled and flew with us. I think Tony jokingly suggested that this would have been a good time to find a new home for them, but I failed to see the humor in that.

Chapter 4

WELCOME TO THE NEIGHBORHOOD

///////////////////

Lauren

Though I knew moving into a new home and building friendships would take some time, I was in for another shock when we arrived in Kansas City. I could not believe the hours Tony and the rest of the coaches were required to work during the season. In Pittsburgh, Chuck Noll had kept his staff at the office as late as 9 p.m. only on an occasional Tuesday night. In Kansas City, Marty kept his coaches working past 1 a.m. Tuesday through Thursday all season long. In fact, sometimes he kept them *way* past one o'clock.

That was one of the toughest adjustments for me. I can remember many nights that first fall when Tony came home at 2 a.m. He would wake me up from a sound sleep, we'd have a short conversation, and then he would want to try to get some rest. I barely saw him, but the kids never saw him during the week. They were asleep when he got home and usually still sleeping when he left for work the next day. So our evenings were a lot different. That's probably why I especially missed the support we'd had at Bethany, our church in Pittsburgh.

One of the reasons, in fact, that Tony had gone to Kansas City early was to get a jump on finding a church. But it didn't turn out that way. We'd been spoiled by seven years at Bethany Baptist with Richard Farmer. He'd been one of the people we'd gone to for help in sorting through our decision, but when we asked him to recommended a church like Bethany in Kansas City, he said he couldn't help because nothing came to his mind.

Finding a church we loved as much as Bethany would be a tough task anyway. We had been at Bethany for our entire marriage. We loved the worship style and the church's small size. The teaching was awesome, and we had grown so much as a couple and as a family.

I wasn't just missing Bethany, though. My entire support system—my parents, sister, brothers, and close friends—were no longer nearby.

TONY

Lauren had been used to talking to her mother all the time. Picking up the phone and calling her had been no big deal in Pittsburgh. Now we were paying long-distance rates. Sometimes I'd just look at the phone bill at the end of the month and shake my head. I'd ask Lauren, "How can we have seven calls to your mom's house on the same day? What could you possibly talk about for that long?"

Lauren may have talked to her mom a lot, but she didn't

live in the past and talk about how she missed Pittsburgh. She was excited about being in a new city and making new friends. Lauren was the one who helped us get comfortable in Kansas City, even before we found a church. She has a remarkable capacity to make friends. She'll meet people anywhere and strike up a conversation. Not only that, she has the discernment to tell almost immediately which people will be a good fit with us. Some of our best friends have come about this way. That is harder for me. I'm too quiet. Like my dad, I guess.

Interestingly, though, Lauren says her relationship with my parents changed while we were in Kansas City. They had always tried to visit us when they could attend home games. They would let us know when they were coming in for the weekend, but we were never sure of what time they would arrive or what their plans were. In Pittsburgh, that had sometimes frustrated Lauren, who felt unprepared. Now that she was away from her family, she was happy anytime our relatives visited!

I think life in Kansas City turned out, in some ways, to be easier for Lauren than in Pittsburgh. More of the coaches were closer in age to us, which allowed her to be a little more comfortable with their wives.

We still knew finding the right church was important though. After a year of visiting various churches, we finally found the right one for us: Paseo Baptist. It was the right size and had great Bible teaching. When Lauren called Pastor Farmer to let him know we'd found a church, he said, "Oh, Paseo Baptist! Charles Briscoe is the pastor. I'd forgotten he is there. He's a great guy, and I've heard that's a great church!"

If only Pastor Farmer had remembered that a year before.

Lauren

Just as at Bethany, we met some special families at Paseo. One of those amazing families was the Besteys. Ulysses and his wife, Augustine, made a tremendous impact on us. Ulysses was an assistant pastor at Paseo, and Augustine was an elementary schoolteacher. We were drawn to this couple because of their love for the Lord and also because they had young children. Ulysses Jr., Mary, and Demetrius were close in age to Tiara and Jamie, so we ended up spending quite a bit of time with their family. We learned from them as we observed how they nurtured and shaped the lives of their children. But the biggest lesson they taught us came after their fourth child, Catherine, was born.

Augustine had experienced a normal pregnancy, so the Besteys were shocked to discover that Catherine had been born blind and with cerebral palsy. Doctors discovered that during her pregnancy Augustine had come in contact with someone with meningitis, which left Catherine with these devastating disabilities. Catherine was not expected to survive her first week.

During this time, Ulysses pointed to Exodus 4:11 as the verse that spoke to them, gave them strength, and held the family together: "Who makes a person's mouth? Who decides whether people speak or do not speak, hear or do not hear, see or do not see? Is it not I, the LORD?"

Ulysses and Augustine didn't know how long Catherine would survive. However, they knew that she had been given to them by God and that their job was to love her and care for her as long as God saw fit. Watching Catherine's parents and siblings shower her with love and affection really spoke to us not only as Christians but as parents. The Besteys demonstrated what unconditional love is all about. Whenever Tony or I was tempted to get frustrated with our children or think about all the work involved in parenting them, we'd think of Ulysses or Augustine proudly carrying Catherine around, giving her the same love and attention as their other three children. And they did it with indescribable joy.

Catherine would never walk or speak. But for the seventeen years she lived, she was a blessing to the Bestey family and to their entire church. The family's attitude toward life and God's sovereignty and faithfulness spoke volumes to us. When we adopted a son with special needs many years later, their example meant even more.

In addition to building new friendships at church, I worked diligently to build relationships with the other coaches' and players' wives and girlfriends. I found it easier to connect with the coaches' wives in Kansas City than in Pittsburgh. While working with the Steelers, Tony and I had been in our mid-twenties. The other coaches and their wives were in their forties and had teenage children. We had been much closer in age to the Steelers' players and their wives. Our friendships with them, however, were somewhat awkward because they viewed Tony as their boss. Now we were closer in age to the other coaches.

It was also easier to connect with the coaches' wives in Kansas City because we were all pretty much in the same boat. We were new to the area and to the Chiefs' organization, and our husbands worked long, demanding hours, so we tried to find things we had in common. We would go to lunch and work out together. It seemed like someone was always pregnant, so we threw lots of showers for one another too. We didn't want to isolate ourselves and get together only on weekends during games. We tried to stay in contact during the week.

Our husbands worked for the team, but we were all involved in the job as well. So working with the Chiefs was like being part of a family. We felt a sense of belonging and would do things together and support one another. I don't know that any of us ever felt lonely or left out because there were always opportunities to get together.

By chance, I also met a couple in our neighborhood who went out of their way to help us get connected. One day as I was pushing Tiara and Jamie in their double stroller, I passed some friendly kids on their bikes. When they biked past us a second time, we stopped and talked for a while. I promised to stop by their house and introduce myself to their parents.

As it turned out, Yvette Morton was one of those "reach-out" persons, the kind who says, "Oh, you're new in the neighborhood? Come on in; you must be hungry. My husband is going to fire up the grill, so you have to stay and eat."

Yvette and her husband, Leo, a phone company executive, wanted to be sure we felt welcome and had been introduced to everybody in the neighborhood. Our family gravitated to their house, where we hung out for hours playing games, watching movies, eating, and just fellowshipping. Yvette was very involved in the community, so she was always encouraging us to join in her events and functions.

Their friendship helped us get to know people and find out about their activities and where they shopped and went to school. Not only did the Mortons help us during our transition, they also provided a good example for us. They believed God wanted them to reach out to others and open their home, especially to young couples. They also encouraged their children to include other children, making them feel welcome. They helped us realize that it's important to embrace new people, and I think we've always tried to do that since that time. Looking back, I'm sometimes amazed at how much the Mortons' willingness to reach out to us impacted our time in that community—and beyond.

I wanted our kids to make other friends, too, and early on, some of the moms in our neighborhood began to get together for weekly playdates with our kids. Many of us were stay-at-home moms whose husbands worked long hours. Visiting parks, the petting zoo, and the children's museum together was also a great way for me to learn my way around the city.

Before long, I felt part of a strong network of friends at church and in the neighborhood, and just as important, my kids were adapting well. I was grateful that Tony had a group of friends who were glad to see him whenever he was able to get away from his office and Arrowhead Stadium.

TONY

Within our first couple of years with the Chiefs, Kansas City had become a special place to all of us. Even my long work hours didn't bother Lauren too much since she and the kids were so busy building friendships.

That's not to say, though, that those years were entirely problem free. We discovered, as all couples do, that even when you're cruising down the road of life, at some point you have to slow down and pull off because of a roadblock ahead—or, as in my case, because of flashing lights in your rearview mirror.

On this particular weeknight, I was driving home from the office sometime after 2 a.m., which was typical during the season. I knew everyone at the house would have fallen asleep long before, and the thought that I would have to leave the house again before the kids woke up was discouraging. At the same time, I knew life could be like that at times.

As I exited Interstate 435 and approached Metcalf Avenue, the light turned red. Once it changed and I made a left to head into our neighborhood, I suddenly noticed flashing lights in my rearview mirror. My heart sank as my pulse picked up. *What in the world? Is a policeman stopping me?*

I pulled over and waited for the officer. He came near the window but kept his distance.

I thought he looked wary as he said, "I was following you on the highway. You were going too fast. Extremely fast. And you didn't signal your turn when you got off the exit. May I see your license and registration?"

It was late, and I was frustrated. I didn't think I had been speeding. I thought, *If I was going "extremely fast," why didn't he stop me on the highway?* I hadn't signaled because I was driving in a lane marked "Exit Only." And it was so late there was no one else on the road anyway! I was upset, but my parents had taught me the biblical admonition to obey the government and its authority. So even though I was anxious to get home, I was going to be patient and cooperative.

But then things changed. After looking at my license, the officer asked me where I worked. In that moment, I went from upset to outraged. He could see from the address on my license that I lived in the neighborhood, and I felt as if he was really asking what I did that enabled me to afford to live here. I simply replied, "I work at the stadium." I wasn't going to say that I was a coach for the Chiefs. By now I believed the only reason he stopped me was because he saw a black face in the car turning into a predominantly white area at that light on Metcalf Avenue.

I was surprised that this thought had even crossed my mind. I wasn't raised to look for prejudice in other people. At times friends had protested that, as a high-profile athlete and coach, I didn't understand what it was like for many black men in America. And that was true. I probably hadn't experienced many of the things they had. It had been a long time since I had thought anyone was treating me differently because of the color of my skin, but that night I definitely did.

The officer said he was going to "give me a break" and write me a ticket only for an improper lane change. At that point I just wanted to get home and didn't say another word, but I knew I was going to contest this ticket.

Once I'd cooled off a bit, Lauren and I discussed the incident and whether I should simply pay the fine. In the end, we agreed that I needed to appeal it since I didn't think I'd done anything wrong. So I headed to traffic court at the time listed on the citation. After hearing my side and listening to the officer's version, the judge found me guilty, but reduced the fine to five dollars. He may have thought that would satisfy me, but I still wasn't happy.

"Wait, does that mean you're finding me guilty?" I asked the judge. "Will this go as a violation on my driving record?"

He shrugged. "Yes, but I'm only fining you five dollars."

He was trying to throw me an olive branch, and perhaps I should have accepted this as a victory. But by now it had become a matter of principle to me. "I didn't do anything wrong. I'm not guilty. I'm not going to pay this fine, so what do I need to do?" I asked.

"Mr. Dungy, you can pay the fine or you can appeal my verdict." He told me the time to appeal—seven or ten days; I can't remember now. I left the courtroom annoyed but convinced that I was not guilty.

For the next couple of days, I mulled the situation over in my mind and talked about my options with Lauren. Should I just send in the five dollars or go through the headache—and the expense—of hiring a lawyer and going to another hearing? Then after working more of those long nights and trying to figure out how to win games, I simply forgot about the ticket.

Until officers showed up at our home one Saturday afternoon. I was there with Lauren and our two children when the doorbell rang.

I answered the door.

"Tony Dungy?"

"Yes."

"You're under arrest." The officers took me to the station and put me in a jail cell for about three hours as I went through the process of entering a plea to the charge of failing to answer a citation. Suddenly, paying the five dollars seemed like a good idea.

I posted the bond and was eventually released. In the meantime, Lauren was upset and had two terrified children on her hands who had witnessed me being taken from the house in a police car. When I got home, we sat the kids down and explained exactly what had happened.

It gave us a chance to talk with them about a lot of things— about the importance of standing up for what you believe and the appropriate response to racial prejudice. But I also had to talk about following the rules and obeying authority. Eventually

I decided to let it go and pay the fine. Unfortunately it was now the original amount plus court costs. It was a surprising—and memorable—lesson for all of us.

Lauren

As devastating as that situation was, overall our family felt so much positive energy in this new environment that even Tony's grueling schedule seemed manageable. He was gone so much during the season that I had to multitask and run the household during those six months. I'd deal with all the bills and mail, decide what repairs needed to be made and who would make them, and be sure the kids finished their homework and got to bed on time. Then off-season would come, and Tony would just step right back in, expecting that the household would work the way that it had worked in Pittsburgh. Except that I'd been running things for the last six months, and we were functioning fine.

Part of the challenge was that Tony felt such pressure to reconnect with the kids when he could. He'd be more inclined to let them stay up for an extra thirty minutes so he could spend time with them, while I'd had them on a schedule. So they loved when Tony was home in the evenings because he'd let them stay up, take them out for ice cream on a school night, or do other fun things. He was constantly getting the routine off-track, though he meant well.

One thing we agreed on, though, was that we had to make the most of those off-season months, reconnecting as a family and enjoying time together. In fact, Tony stopped playing golf in Kansas City because he felt he couldn't justify spending five hours of free time by himself, without me and the kids.

Instead, we spent many days with friends at Oceans of Fun and Worlds of Fun, two amusement parks owned by Lamar Hunt, the owner of the Chiefs. All of the coaching staff had been given complimentary family passes to the attractions. We thought it was the greatest thing in the world to pack coolers and take the kids to Oceans of Fun, where we'd enjoy being in the water and the sun for hours.

We began taking car trips in the summer as well. Off-season began in February, the middle of winter. As soon as it began to get warm, though, we were on the go. In fact, our kids just got used to jumping in the car and going places from a very young age. We piled our luggage on top in a "turtle" luggage carrier and drove everywhere. The teacher in me wouldn't allow the kids to lose their academic skills in the summer, so in addition to singing songs and playing games in the car, I helped them brush up on their academic skills by having them keep journals, drawing pictures of what they saw and doing Hooked on Phonics with them.

One summer, we made our first trip to Black Mountain, North Carolina, to a Fellowship of Christian Athletes conference. They run an outstanding camp for coaches' families, which not only gave our kids time to enjoy the outdoors but also to get some great spiritual teaching. We also took car trips with the kids to see my parents in Pittsburgh or Tony's in Michigan.

We realized that, as important as it was to spend time as a family with Tiara and Jamie, we also had to carve out time for the two of us. We couldn't be together as much as we'd like, so we needed to make the times we were together count. So we started walking together for thirty to forty minutes at the end of the day as a way to stay in contact with each other. We walked together as much as possible, though usually just on

Friday nights during the season. Not only was it great exercise, but it gave us a fixed time to communicate—to be away from all distractions. Many times we would put the kids in bed and then walk and talk about what had been going on at work or at home, or about what we hoped to do in the next couple of days. When the kids were still little we couldn't walk around the whole neighborhood and always kept our house in sight, but as Tiara got older, we were gradually able to lengthen the time we walked. There was little traffic in our neighborhood, and we both looked forward to our time alone.

TONY

This is a habit we've continued ever since. For us, especially when I became a head coach, walking was easier than going out to dinner or going out in public. We could talk without interruption and without anyone stopping us or sitting down with us to start a conversation.

We also started doing more bike riding in Overland Park, which had miles of bike trails running through parks, wooded areas, and along streams. Once we realized we wanted to get more serious about bike riding during my first off-season, we decided to replace the older, uncomfortable bikes we'd brought with us from Pittsburgh with newer models. When I explained to the bike salesman what I was looking for, he recommended I buy a pair of Specialized Hardrocks. After looking at the price tag, I went home in a daze. I told Lauren about the bikes and then told her they cost $275 each, which was more than I'd paid for my first car! Lauren talked me out of buying cheaper ones, pointing out that they wouldn't hold up as long and we'd be paying for quality and durability.

I'm so much like my dad, I guess, that it was hard for me to agree to buy the better bikes. I have to say Lauren was right. Those Hardrocks were great. I should say they *are* great. Twenty-five years later, we still ride them, and every one of our kids has enjoyed the view from the kid's seat on the back of our bikes. I guess you do get what you pay for.

I learned to defer to Lauren in another area: entertaining. One reason I think Lauren enjoyed the Mortons so much was that God has definitely given her the gift of hospitality. She loves to plan and entertain, abilities that I have come to appreciate over the years. Sometimes when she was getting ready for guests early on in our marriage, I'd say, "We don't need that much food" or "Why do we have to move *all* the furniture around?" She'd simply respond, "Trust me."

At one time, such exchanges frustrated me because her plans weren't always the way I would want to do things. Yet after every party was over and I'd watched our guests enjoying themselves, I knew Lauren was right. I've found it's best to listen to her and not get bent out of shape when we're getting ready for company. I'm happy that she does all the planning and I simply do the legwork.

I've watched some men get annoyed when their wives take the lead in any area of their homes. I think that's shortsighted. As Chuck Noll used to tell his coaches, our job was to help the players play the best they could. So I can't look at my marriage and think, *My job is to be the head coach and make the rules, and Lauren's job is to make sure my rules are being followed.* No, our job in marriage is to help the house function as well as it can and to raise our kids in the best way possible.

Though Kansas City ended up being a great place for our

family to grow together, it was close to three years before we actually grew in size. That would happen in January 1992, when we had just finished our third season with the Chiefs after losing to the Buffalo Bills in the playoffs the week before. So instead of being in Denver, coaching in the AFC Championship against the Broncos, I found myself that Sunday in the delivery room, waiting for our third child to be born. Of course, as we watched the championship game in the hospital room while we were waiting on our new son, I assured Lauren that even had we won the week before, I would have been right there with her.

But times were different back then. There was a lot of pressure to be there on the job, no matter what. People weren't as understanding about family issues. I *think* I would have been there. Had we beaten Buffalo, though, I know that I would have been in some deep prayer asking God to allow the baby to come before the weekend!

Even though we'd been knocked out of the playoffs, it was a wonderful, joyous time for us. We had a new baby, a network of good friends, and another great church. But the Lord was about to shake our lives up once again. As we held our newborn, Eric Anthony, for the first time, we had no idea that in less than a month changes at work would lead us to pull up stakes and move once again.

Chapter 5
INTO THE COLD

////////////////////

TONY

Few years seemed to begin with more promise than 1992. A newborn always adds excitement to a home, and Tiara and Jamie were thrilled to have a little brother. On top of that, my old boss with the Steelers, Chuck Noll, had retired, and the Chiefs' defensive coordinator, Bill Cowher, left our staff to replace him in Pittsburgh. Marty had always told me that if Bill ever left, I would get the job of defensive coordinator. I was sure Bill's departure meant that I was in line for a promotion. This was going to be perfect!

Now, just as I was prepared to jump into that position, Denny Green contacted me. Denny had recently been named head coach of the Minnesota Vikings. I knew him from my days playing for the 49ers, when he had coached the wide receivers. He was calling to see if I had any interest in coming to Minnesota as his defensive coordinator.

I had no plans to go to Minnesota, but before I turned him down I thought I should let Marty know that the Vikings had called. It couldn't hurt my contract negotiations if he knew someone else was interested in me.

After telling Marty about Denny's call, I was shocked when Marty said I should check out Minnesota. That's a pretty bad sign, I've learned. When your boss suggests that you might want to look at opportunities elsewhere, you should probably do so. And I couldn't help but think of a remark Lauren had made to me late in the season. Although our family had enjoyed a close relationship with the Schottenheimers (he insisted that my kids call him Uncle Marty), Lauren said she felt as if something about our friendship with them was off. We lived in the subdivision next to theirs and had enjoyed many pool dates and lunches at their house. After giving her a lovely baby shower, however, Marty's wife, Pat, seemed to be avoiding Lauren. Marty wasn't the same friendly, approachable coach we had known him to be either. But then again Lauren thought that maybe her concerns were simply the result of her being more sensitive after recently having a baby.

I would never have gone up to Minnesota for the interview if Marty hadn't suggested it. I was still a little naive, I guess, because I thought if the interview went well, I would actually be able to choose between the two jobs. Denny knew that one of the keys to getting me would be convincing Lauren, so he invited her to come with me.

I told Lauren this would be a free trip for her and an opportunity to visit my brother, Linden, and his wife, Donna. We'd spend just one night there before returning to Kansas the following day.

The bitterly cold weekend did nothing to endear Lauren to Minnesota, but at that point I wasn't too concerned because I assumed we would be going back with the Chiefs. Even so, the Vikings had lined up a realtor to drive Lauren around and look at homes while I met with Denny.

At the end of our meeting, Denny offered me the job. As soon as I was back in Kansas City, I told Marty the details. I may have been secretly hoping there would be a bidding war and I'd get a nice raise. But I knew that even if the Vikings offered me a little more, I was going to stay in Kansas City.

What neither Lauren nor I realized was that Marty had quietly hired Dave Adolph of the Raiders to be the Chiefs' new defensive coordinator. Dave had been Cleveland's defensive coordinator when Marty was the Browns' coach several years before. The two men were close friends.

Only after I'd told Marty about the Vikings' offer did my boss tell me that he had hired Dave. Marty said he wanted me to stay in my same position but would understand if I took the Vikings' job.

At that moment I was hurt because I felt that Marty had not been honest with me. Then I got mad. I didn't ask him any questions. I told him I would think it over, but when I left that office I had no desire to go back to work for the Chiefs.

Staying with Kansas City wasn't an option for me at that point, and I was glad that I had the chance to go with the Vikings. Otherwise, I'm not sure what I would have done. I might have had to take a demotion to go anywhere else. Even after I had a chance to calm down a little, I was determined to go somewhere, and Minnesota was the best option at the time.

Looking back, I think Marty wishes he hadn't made any promises to me in the beginning. And if he hadn't promised me the position, maybe I would have stayed in Kansas City. I had much more empathy for Marty once I became a head coach. That was a lesson for me, and as a result, I tried not to promise anything to my coaches if I wasn't absolutely certain I could deliver. Marty and I remain friends to this day because I don't hold a grudge against him for what happened. I think it was God's way of moving us on and getting us prepared for what He had in store for us later.

On that day, though, I was still angry when I got home, and I was pretty matter-of-fact with Lauren. I told her we were going to Minnesota because Marty had hired someone else for the position he had promised me.

Lauren

The events of January 1992 remain as troubling as any we've gone through. Well, maybe that's a little too strong.

They still don't sit well with me, anyway. That's when the phrase "the NFL means 'Not for Long'" was driven home for me in a personal way. And I was very hurt because I felt like I'd been left completely out of that decision-making process. Despite the attempts Tony and I had made to take regular walks together, the in-season hours—especially during the playoffs—had finally taken their toll, and I was caught off guard. Communication had simply broken down at a most critical time.

To be honest, while Tony was waiting for word of a promotion from Marty, I didn't give it much thought. I just assumed that when Bill left, Tony would get the job. After all, when he hired Tony, Marty had said that he wouldn't bring in someone before moving up a coach who was already there. On top of that, I had plenty to focus on with a new baby at home. Jamie was five years old, so it had been a while since we had a baby in the house.

When Tony asked me to visit Denny in Minnesota with him, I was not at all excited to go. I knew Tony wasn't going to take the job even if it was offered to him. We were expecting his promotion, we were settled at a phenomenal church, and we were living in a wonderful neighborhood. Our children were happy at their schools, and we had support and unbelievable friendships with other Christian families. But I agreed to accompany Tony to Minnesota so he and Denny could talk. I bundled up eight-day-old Eric in his newborn snowsuit and off we went.

As we taxied into Minneapolis, the pilot announced that the temperature was minus four degrees. Just then I noticed Tony divert his eyes to his briefcase to avoid eye contact with me. I'm sure he was thinking that the frigid weather and the fact that I was fresh out of the hospital after childbirth were not making this an ideal start to the visit.

To show you how out of touch we were at that point: as I got off the plane with Tony and our brand-new baby, I remember holding Eric close to me, protecting him from the Arctic winds, as I kept saying to myself, *Glad we don't live here; glad we're in just for the weekend 'cause it's too bitterly cold, and it's too far.*

Denny's secretary kept Eric in his car seat in her office as we visited with Denny. Denny had arranged for a real estate agent to show me around the city. As the realtor drove us around scenic Lake Minnetonka, I did see some beautiful homes and some gorgeous properties. But I also saw people sitting in huts on the frozen lake *ice fishing*! This might have been the wondrous "land of ten thousand lakes," but it was not a place where I envisioned living and raising a family.

When I returned to the Viking complex, Tony and Denny were wrapping up their meeting, and I noticed there were contract papers sitting on the table. This was a very low point in my life because I felt the communication between Tony and me had broken down to the point where we definitely weren't on the same page. Why weren't we praying about this situation together? Why did I feel left out of the discussion?

I was hurt and didn't understand what was going on. One day he was "just talking" with Denny, and the next thing I knew, Tony had agreed to take the Vikings job and was signing his name on the contract. I was thinking, *Oh my goodness—wait, wait; what happened?* I felt so overlooked during the process.

And it wasn't that I didn't trust Tony. That wasn't it at all. He's always been a man of God. He's always prayed before making decisions. He is always looking out for our interests. I trust him—completely—and I did then. I just felt . . . left out.

I'm sure Tony tried to share his thoughts with me, but it wasn't until much later that I started to understand how he felt. At the moment he told me we were moving to Minnesota, though, I was in shock. How could I appreciate what he hadn't discussed with me? I had no idea what was going on other than all of a sudden Tony said we were leaving. I didn't know the whole story.

Communication is so important in a marriage. Talking about things is the only way to be sure you're always in sync. I don't know if it was the heavy workload during the season or maybe that we were talking more about the new baby coming. I'm not sure, but in this case we wound up on very different pages.

TONY

I really did think I was communicating. And even though Denny had a contract ready for me and wanted me to accept the job on the spot, I didn't. I wanted to be in Kansas City. It was only after talking it over with Marty that I determined I couldn't stay, and I felt that Lauren couldn't appreciate what had happened to the working relationship with my boss.

I had lost the trust factor with Marty, and it would have been hard for me to put my all into the job at that point. With all the hours we worked and the way I had to shortchange Lauren and the kids during the season . . . I felt that I had been a loyal employee and hadn't gotten that loyalty in return. It was a matter of principle to me.

And to Lauren's credit, even though she wasn't fired up about the move, she did everything she could to make it work. She contacted the realtors and began the process of getting the house market-ready while I flew to Minneapolis the next week and began my new job. In the meantime, I was doing everything I could to be helpful.

I drove back on the weekends, leaving work on Fridays at 3 p.m. and getting into Overland Park at 11 p.m. I spent Saturdays with Lauren and the kids, and then I drove back to Minnesota right after church each Sunday. That was my routine almost every weekend from mid-January to June. I wore out all my Michael W. Smith and BeBe and CeCe Winans cassette tapes driving up and down I-35 those six months.

Thankfully, when I was in Minnesota, my work hours were much better than they had been, which made my weekend commute much more tolerable. I was also enjoying my job as the Vikings' defensive coordinator, which brought new players, new coaches, and new challenges. I had a lot more responsibility, but I was able to leave the office so much earlier. I couldn't wait to be reunited with Lauren and our kids, knowing I would have much more time to enjoy our family. My brother and his family lived nearby, and I was looking forward to our kids growing up with their cousins.

Lauren

As sad as I was about leaving Kansas City, I missed Tony during the week and looked forward to being together again. Putting our house on the market and trying to sell it quickly presented challenges, however. Our house was listed in February, typically not a good time of the year to show a home. Also, while our house was only three years old and in great condition, we were competing against a lot of new construction. New subdivisions were popping up all over, and it was a buyer's market.

In spite of the competition, our realtor was confident that she could sell our home quickly. I sure hoped so, since during this time, I had to keep the household in Kansas City running, help the kids with their schoolwork, and care for an infant.

Tony and I wanted to get settled in Minnesota as soon as possible, so we took another step of faith and started building a house there even before our Kansas City house had sold.

The architecture in Kansas City, which had seemed so new to us when we moved in, had really grown on us. We loved it so much that Tony and I asked our builder to design our new home based on our Kansas City floor plans. Our builder wasn't familiar with some of the concepts, but after we showed them to him, he was excited to try them. We put the older kids' bedrooms on the lower level. Eric would have a room upstairs with us. The main floor had a nice hearth-room kitchen with a huge deck off the family room. Our new home was finished in mid-June, a month before our house in Kansas City ended up selling. As soon as school was out, the kids and I headed up to Minnesota.

I had to admit that Minnesota was beautiful in the summer—so much different than it had been in January. Jamie and Tiara were excited to have their own space, and I was trying my best to get excited too. *Maybe—just maybe—this might work after all.*

But I soon discovered that although the area where we lived was beautiful and Tony's working conditions were great, we were going to face a new set of challenges.

When the kids and I joined Tony in Minnesota, many of the coaches were leaving for their vacations, so I wouldn't have the opportunity to meet or connect with any of the wives until the fall football season started. On top of that, I soon learned that most of the Vikings players didn't live in Minnesota full time. That meant their wives and families weren't around either.

The structure of the organization was quite different too. The Chiefs' owner, Lamar Hunt, and Marty and Pat Schottenheimer had been big on family. They always seemed to have events going on for the staff. The Vikings were owned by a group of ten people, so it wasn't the same. The Vikings coach, Denny Green, was very personable, and he always went out of his way for me and the kids. But because he wasn't married at the time, there was no head coach's wife to organize functions. That made it difficult to build the closeness with the other wives that I'd become accustomed to. So even though Tony was around more, I was lonelier without the connection to the people at his job.

Forging friendships in our new neighborhood was more challenging too. In Overland Park, we had moved into a brand-new subdivision, and we got to know each new family as they moved in. In Minnesota, we moved into an established neighborhood, so we *were* the new people. Our neighbors were friendly but very set in their own routines and relationships.

I tried to stay positive, though, and look on the bright side. It was good having Tony's brother and his family nearby. They lived about thirty-five minutes away from us, and I loved it whenever the kids were able to get together. I had always wanted our children to grow up around family the way I had.

In addition, when I visited the neighborhood schools, I discovered they were excellent. The schools in the Eden Prairie area, where we lived, consistently received A ratings. Tiara and Jamie were going to love them.

I did develop one close friendship that first year, and it was all through God's providence. A group of my friends in Kansas City were shopping at a mall when they spotted an adorable baby in one of the stores. They struck up a conversation with the mom, who told them her name was Alene Buonomo. Her family, she said, was in the process of moving back to Minnesota. My friends told Alene that I was moving to Minnesota and might need some help getting acclimated once I got there.

Although she didn't know any of us, Alene gave my friends her number and told them to have me call when I got to Minnesota. When I called Alene, I quickly found out that she was as warm and personable as my friends said, and I also discovered we had a lot in common. She and her husband, Pete, had two young children, and they were looking to develop relationships with other Christian families. We hit it off right away and have remained close friends to this day.

It wasn't happenstance that my friends noticed a cute baby in the mall. No, I believe it was God providing me with a close relationship that I would desperately need during that initial year in Minnesota.

Chapter 6

SPOUSAL SUPPORT

/////////////////.

Lauren

We'd been in Minnesota only a short time when I first heard about the Halloween snowstorm the year before. The snow started flying on October 31, and by the time the storm had ended, the Twin Cities had been dumped with twenty-eight inches of snow. The Vikings were so concerned that their players might not make it to the complex safely that they canceled practice.

I shivered just hearing that story. Wintertime was when it got especially tough for me. I grew up in Pittsburgh—not exactly a tropical locale—but this was a different kind of winter. So cold and so long. When the temperature dropped below zero, it was difficult to go out. We had to warm up our car for fifteen minutes in the garage before heading out. And it got dark so early.

When I met the kids at the school bus at 4 p.m., many nearby homes already had their porch lights on.

The most challenging time came when the season was over in January and so many Vikings deserted the town for warmer weather. All the players' wives and many of the coaches' wives flew out right after the last game. I was especially lonely when Tony had to leave to go on extended scouting trips. I know he felt guilty whenever he'd have to tell me in February or March that he was going to Arizona State or the University of Miami!

Not only couldn't I build camaraderie with the wives of other Viking players and coaches, I missed the community we'd enjoyed at church. Finding a church took us much longer than it had in Kansas City—our search lasted almost three years, in fact. People say you shouldn't church hop, that you should make a commitment and stick to it. However, in addition to offering sound biblical teaching, which was our number one priority, our church needed to be our place of refuge, especially in the off-season. And we needed a place where we could build strong relationships. So the church had to be just right, or we would keep looking.

Nothing seemed to measure up to what we'd had at Bethany in Pittsburgh. Tony and I were looking for that perfect church, and we found ourselves comparing everything to what we were used to. We'd say things like "This service is too long." "That pastor is too formal." "This church is too large." "That one is too far, and it doesn't have an established children's program." Most of all, I was looking for a place where I could build relationships. You know, not a church where I'd go only on Sundays, but where I could go to Bible studies and other activities during the week.

Finding the right church has been one of the toughest parts of all our moves. But it's so important for us that we weren't going to give up. Another challenge in Minnesota was that Tony was no longer an anonymous assistant coach. In addition to being the defensive coordinator of the Vikings, he was somewhat of a hometown hero, having played quarterback for the University of Minnesota. And while it was great to be recognized and welcomed, we were rarely able to come into a new church and be treated as a normal family that was there to worship.

I tried to keep a good attitude by staying busy with the kids and their activities. It definitely was a challenge. The biggest lesson I learned was that complaining wasn't the way to go. In this instance, I had no reason to assign fault to Tony for my unhappiness. In fact, we've learned that it's not always necessary to figure out who is wrong when we disagree. Instead, we try to think about an issue from the other person's point of view. Then we talk about how to resolve a situation in the best way—which is not necessarily my way or Tony's way.

The toughest situations are when we have a difference of opinion and there's really no right or wrong answer. One of the biggest decisions of our marriage was whether to stay in Kansas City or go to Minnesota. What did we do when we didn't agree?

When Tony and I don't view a situation in the same way, I believe I have to follow what the Bible says about marital roles and let Tony know, "I feel strongly about this, but we're going to do what you think is best. As the husband and father of our home, you bear the primary responsibility to lead in our home."

That doesn't mean I stuff down my feelings or put on an

artificial smile. I am open with Tony about my disappointment, but I don't allow myself to hang on to bitterness or resentment. I believe this approach works for us because Tony is committed to loving me sacrificially as the Bible commands husbands to love their wives. That means he listens to me, values my opinions, and treats me with sensitivity and respect.

In Minnesota, I learned that Tony and I had to work through issues and come up with ways that we could make our new hometown fun. I was still on the lookout for couples to connect with, and anytime I saw someone with kids our age, I struck up a conversation. It could be at school, the grocery store, or the health club. It didn't matter.

I met Maria Moran and Noella Gordon at Tiara's elementary school. They lived close to us and had children who were the same ages as our kids. Once Tony got to know their husbands, our families quickly bonded and we began doing family activities together on the weekends. The Morans introduced us to camping, and our three families took several end-of-the-school-year trips to Whitewater State Park in southeastern Minnesota.

We enjoyed camping so much that we began considering an invitation we'd been given shortly after we moved to Minnesota. Sheldon Burns, one of the Vikings' team physicians, told us about his cabin up north that, due to his schedule, he was able to use only a couple of times a year. He invited our family to stay at his cabin whenever we wanted.

During our first three years with the Vikings, we never went. As cold as I was most of the time, I just couldn't imagine going farther north! Finally, though, we decided to take Dr. Burns up on his offer and visit his cabin for a weekend. The location was absolutely stunning. His cabin backed up to a lake with majestic scenery all around. We took the kids tubing and hiking in the woods. We cooked out a number of times. After our wonderful weekend, I couldn't believe we hadn't taken advantage of his cabin before. I knew I had no one but myself and my preconceived notions to blame.

In fact, I was coming to realize that the Lord had been testing my faith throughout our years in Minnesota. Tony had had some disappointments in his career, but this was really the first time I struggled with discouragement. I had to rely on God for His peace of mind during these challenging times.

I think what helped me most was what I was learning in my Bible Study Fellowship class. I had heard about BSF in Kansas City but didn't start attending until I got to Minnesota. I loved meeting weekly with other women who wanted to learn and grow by studying the Bible. We had a great discussion leader who made the lessons come alive. It was so exciting that many times I would go directly to the Vikings' complex after our study and enthusiastically share what I had learned with Tony over lunch.

Tony was so impressed that he began leaving work on Mondays in time to go to the BSF men's group that met at about eight. Then he'd catch up on any work he needed to do the next morning.

At BSF, we often talked about finding the blessings in the midst of disappointments and how the Lord was always working in our lives. Those truths opened my eyes. I realized that I was still complaining a lot and wasn't appreciative of all that I had to be grateful and thankful for. That, I think, is when I started to understand that God could use me even in the cold of Minnesota if I was willing to let Him.

Without question, one of the things I could be grateful for was getting to spend more time with Tony in the evenings. That was a welcome change for both me and our kids. Tiara and Jamie were at the ages when they wanted to tell us all about their days. And that was important. We started having family meetings where they could tell us what was going on in their lives and we could talk through issues: "I liked seeing your sportsmanship at the game" or "Hey, you guys aren't doing your chores" or "You did an awesome job on your schoolwork."

We also talked about activities we might want to do as a family and asked the kids to give some input into the planning. As they got involved with more after-school activities, it was a good time to go over schedules and determine who needed to be where the next day. That was probably most critical when it came to planning for the weekends. Between out-of-town company, kids' activities, and the games, our weekends were even busier than our weekdays.

In the midst of busy schedules and kids dominating dinner-table conversations, Tony and I knew that it was important to find some time to be alone together without feeling like we were neglecting the kids. That's when those walks and bike rides became even more important than they'd been in Kansas City.

We actually walked more in Minnesota despite the weather. Or maybe it was because of the weather; we did more walking and less bike riding in the cold. We didn't have fenced-in property, and we knew that the dogs needed to get out. I actually looked forward to starting out on our two-and-a-half-mile walking loop, which gave us about forty minutes to talk. During football season, we knew it would be hard to fit it in, but we always did.

Slowly, I grew to be more patient and at peace about where God had us. That was especially helpful a few years later when Tony was anxious to find a head coaching position but nothing seemed to open up for him. I didn't know all the ins and outs of football, but I knew that Tony was more than qualified for a head coaching job. Other coaches we knew were advancing, and I couldn't help but wonder why Tony wasn't getting that chance. Looking back, I think God used the whole process to help our faith grow.

Now don't misunderstand: I still wanted to leave Minnesota and move to—well, anywhere that was warmer and closer to my family. But I knew we needed to let God direct us and not try to make that move happen ourselves.

Looking back, I realize there was a lot working against us in Minnesota. Sometimes you never know where you'll find your tests as a couple. And this was a test. For the first time in our ten years of marriage, our emotions and perceptions didn't line up.

TONY

Lauren is right. While she found it hard to adjust to Minnesota, I was really enjoying life there. The Vikings got off to a great start my first season, and the defense played well. The players were responding to me, and the fans were energized. On top of that, I loved working for Denny. And the hours were *so* much better. I was home earlier at night and felt much more refreshed when I was around.

I used to call Herm Edwards, who had been promoted to my job in Kansas City, when I was leaving work at nine o'clock to tease him, knowing that he probably had four or five hours left at the office. Sometimes I would have Jamie draw the diagrams on my play cards that we would use in the next day's practice, so as soon as we got the game plan set I would come home and let Jamie start drawing them. Those nights, I might come home at 7:30.

As much as I enjoyed being back in Minnesota, where I'd also gone to college, I knew Lauren wasn't as happy as I was. I think I was sensitive to that, but the frustrating thing was I didn't know what to do to help.

I came to realize that I needed to be there more for Lauren. It was really weird because, in so many ways, Minnesota was a better situation for our family. The time requirement was so much lighter and the stress level so much less that I felt I could be a better husband and father.

With Denny, we always had the same schedule, which was great for the assistants, because we could really plan our family life. And because he had no problems with us bringing the kids to the office, Jamie became a regular visitor. I'd even take him to practice with me on days he didn't have school. Jamie loved being around the players, and pretty soon he felt like he was part of the team.

My nightly walks with Lauren were a critical time for me to find out what had happened during her day and what was going on with the kids at school. I also tried to share with her what was going on at work, especially any frustrations I might have. For the first two years there weren't many, but eventually one thing did start to get to me: not getting an opportunity to be a head coach.

I had worked for three great head coaches and had learned a lot from each one. I felt I was ready to run my own team, but it didn't look like the opportunity was going to come any time soon—especially after the 1993 season, our second year in Minnesota.

Even though we had the number one defense in the NFL that year and there were seven head coaching openings, not one of those teams called me to interview. At that point I actually thought I might never get a head coaching job. But Lauren encouraged me to be patient, reminding me that the Lord was in control and that the right situation was going to come.

A lot of people felt it was a racial issue, that the NFL was still not giving African American coaches fair opportunities to advance. I thought that was true but also believed that the perception of me as a person had a lot to do with it. Many people in the NFL viewed me as being too nice, too mild-mannered to succeed as a head coach. In some of the interviews I'd had with owners, I had been asked how I would be able to motivate players without yelling at them or using profanity. My Christian beliefs didn't necessarily fit the image many owners and general managers had of a head coach. I knew I would never change the way I approached coaching and would never back off from my principles, so I wasn't sure what the future held.

The next two off-seasons were emotional roller coasters, for sure. And a lot of our frustration came from the interviews I *didn't* have. A newspaper article would say that a certain team was interested in Tony Dungy, but I would have to tell Lauren that I had not heard anything from that team. She'd say, "Why don't you call them and apply for the job?" In the NFL, if you have to apply, you're not going to get the job. They have to want you.

Finally, in 1994, there came a couple of head coaching opportunities for which I was being seriously considered—Philadelphia and Jacksonville. Of the two, Philly was a little more intense, since I interviewed, talked on the phone with the team's leadership, and then went back for a second interview. Jeffrey Lurie, the team's owner, told me what he was looking for in a head coach, and I thought I fit the bill perfectly.

I was disappointed to come in number two for that position. Getting so close but not landing the job was difficult for both of us, but maybe even tougher on Lauren. For that reason, she didn't allow herself to get her hopes up about the Jacksonville position. And as it turned out, I interviewed only once with them. During our discussion, I realized I probably wouldn't get the job. They were looking for someone to run the whole operation—to be both general manager and head coach—and I preferred to concentrate on the coaching. And I'm not sure they were convinced I would be committed enough to the job, as I explained how my faith and my family were so important to me. But they still told me that I was in the running and that they'd call me at home in the next forty-eight hours with their decision. When we hadn't heard anything during that time, we knew the job was going to someone else. It's easy now to see what God's plan was and how well it turned out for us, but at the time these were major disappointments.

Instead of thinking that I was getting closer to a head coaching position, doubts started creeping in. I couldn't help but wonder, *Is it ever going to happen?* Vikings chaplain Tom Lamphere counseled me to keep my eyes on Christ and to be the best assistant coach I could be. He told me to follow the Lord's guidance and not worry about everything else. "Put it in God's hands," he said.

So as I went into the 1995 season, I tried not to focus on my disappointment over the two head coaching opportunities I didn't get. Instead, I got back to work with the goal of helping our team get to the Super Bowl. Yet at times I couldn't help but wonder about my chances of becoming a head coach.

Letdowns like that are why God gave me a good wife. I needed to hear Lauren tell me that she loved me and believed in me no matter what. And that's what she did.

Lauren

As Tony prepared to head to training camp at the end of July, I decided to take the kids to visit my parents before we got back into the grind of the season. Though it would be an eighteen-hour trip by car, I knew I wouldn't mind the driving. I'd made many long car trips with the kids and always looked forward to putting on teaching sermons after they settled down and went to sleep. I knew I'd be inspired by the powerful messages as I drove.

What I did feel nervous about, though, was the idea of stopping late at night to try finding a hotel. I was never comfortable when my kids and I had to stay in a strange hotel without Tony. When he offered to make a hotel reservation for us somewhere in Ohio, I said no. "Ohio? Why, I'll practically be home by then."

When I packed for our trip, I included plenty of supplies for the kids—coloring books, crafts, music, and snacks. We had a great time, laughing, talking, and singing as I drove—that is, until we got to Sandusky, Ohio, at about 11 p.m.

By that time, I realized we still had two and a half hours to go. Tiara and Jamie had fallen asleep, Anne Graham Lotz's message on Revelation was over, and I was starting to get really sleepy. Had I been able, I would have called Tony and told him I'd take him up on that hotel offer now. But I had no cell phone and was too fearful to look for and then stop at a phone booth. I just prayed and kept driving.

As I did, God sent a miracle. Out of nowhere, three-year-old Eric popped his head up from the backseat and said, "Mom, how are you doing? Are you okay?"

To this day I don't know why Eric woke up just then, but my precious preschooler, with his high-pitched, squeaky voice, kept up a lively conversation with me all the way to Pittsburgh. When I finally pulled into my parents' driveway, I was beyond exhausted but relieved to be there. And maybe a little more willing to take logical suggestions from my husband in the future!

I went into that fall determined to apply the lessons I was learning in BSF and to live with a Christlike attitude. I was intentional about being joyful and a blessing to my husband, children, and other people, even when I didn't feel like it.

That resolution was made a little easier to keep thanks to my new friendship with Yvette Sherman, whose husband, Ray, had joined Denny's staff as the quarterback coach earlier that year. Yvette's personality is so much like mine. She's an excellent tennis player and doesn't like to lose at anything. We both have that competitive spirit and hit it off immediately.

Like me, Yvette loves entertaining and playing games. Whenever we hosted a party at one of our houses, we always brought out the board games for a matchup between the men and the women. Whether it was Pictionary, Guesstures, cards, or volleyball, Yvette and I made a great team, and we didn't lose to the guys very often.

To help plan my biggest party that fall, however, I turned to the Morans and the Gordons. We would throw a celebration sure to bring back memories from the year Tony and I met.

His birthday happened to coincide with the team's off week, and since he'd be turning forty, it called for a celebration with family and friends. We decided that a surprise celebration at Dr. Burns's cabin would be the perfect way to celebrate his big 4-0!

Once our families had arrived and unpacked, the guys took Tony out to the garage and kept him occupied playing Ping-Pong and pool. The kids, who had been sworn to secrecy, along with Maria, Noella, and I, jumped into action and transformed the family room into party central. We hung "over the hill"–themed banners and balloons, set out party plates and cups on the table, and placed large platters of fried chicken, macaroni and cheese, sweet potatoes, and greens—Tony's favorite foods—on the counters. As we got ready, we began playing old-school music by Al Green, Marvin Gaye, and Aretha Franklin to get us in the mood. Finally, we put on our black attire to commemorate Tony's "old age" and pulled his presents and gag gifts out of hiding.

When everything was ready, one of the kids told Tony he was needed inside. As he walked through the door, cameras started flashing and we all yelled, "Surprise!" The expression on his face said it all. He had been blindsided by another surprise party.

TONY

Lauren *had* surprised me, and once again I had to laugh at how the football season could affect my perception. I had no idea of all the planning that was going on right under my nose.

After that fun getaway weekend, however, I had to get right back to work. The Vikings started the 1995 season with high hopes. Our team was very talented, and I was sure we could be in the hunt for the Super Bowl. Unfortunately, as the season progressed, things weren't gelling as I'd expected. We were playing up and down, and after our first four games, we were 2–2.

The coaches used the bye week to evaluate what we'd been doing and to consider how we could develop more consistency. I was hoping the week off would energize our team, but for as much effort as we put into things, 1995 just didn't seem to be our year. We did not play up to our capabilities. For the first time since Denny Green and his staff had gotten to Minnesota, we missed the playoffs.

My dream of landing a head coaching position didn't look promising either. At the end of that season, not many jobs opened up and only two were viable possibilities: Tampa Bay and Miami. The rumor mill had those two jobs filled as soon as they came open. Jimmy Johnson had coached the Dallas Cowboys to two Super Bowl wins and was an icon in Miami, having led the University of Miami to a national championship. Steve Spurrier, head coach at the University of Florida, was just as well respected and coveted in Tampa. In fact, we had a close friend on the Florida staff who told us they were all preparing to go to Tampa.

I hated to tell Lauren that there was virtually no chance of moving that year. After all, there were two slam-dunk candidates for the two openings. On top of that, the Vikings were coming off a bad year.

Then, unexpectedly, I got a call. I was asked to interview with Rich McKay, the Buccaneers' general manager, in California, where he and I would both be attending the East-West Shrine Game. They weren't even bringing me into Tampa because it was early in the process and they were quietly interviewing candidates. Knowing this, I didn't get my hopes up and warned Lauren that I was a long shot for this position.

The interview began with less promise than even I had expected. That's because as I arrived at the hotel, minutes before our meeting, a screw in my eyeglasses came out and the long piece that fit over my right ear came off. I had no time to get the glasses fixed. *Should I keep them off, or should I use my hands to hold them up?* I wondered.

I finally decided to put on my glasses, thinking Rich might ask me to review some paperwork or diagram a play. I explained my predicament to him and then, as the interview got underway, I held on to the glasses with my right hand to keep them from falling off, which both looked and felt awkward. (In the back of my mind, I could hear Lauren asking me why I hadn't followed her advice to get contacts, or at least a second pair of glasses!)

About halfway through our conversation, Rich told me he wouldn't be asking me to review anything, and said I could take off my glasses. He couldn't have been more gracious during our meeting, but I left feeling like it had been a disaster.

And so, as I flew back home, I began mentally preparing myself for another year in Minnesota.

Chapter 7
A WARM LANDING

///////////////////////

Lauren

One morning after dropping the kids off at school, I decided to head over to the mall. The temperature had fallen to almost twenty below zero overnight, and our city was digging out from another big snowstorm. Like Tony, I had resigned myself to spending another cold, blustery winter in Minnesota, and I wanted to pick up a new electric blanket.

When I got home, I set the blanket control to 9—or maybe even all the way up to 10—and crawled into bed. Within minutes, the warmth began to spread, and I felt as if my body was finally thawing out. *It's another bitterly cold day in Minnesota,* I thought. *I can't even convince myself to meet Yvette at the health club to swim laps. I'm just going to take a nap.*

As I was dozing off, our second phone line rang. Only Tony

used that line, so I knew he was calling. I assumed he was just checking in, so I didn't move. I figured Tony would either hang up or leave a message.

But the phone kept ringing and ringing. I finally dove out from underneath the blanket and picked up the receiver. Tony was whispering on the other end, and I couldn't hear much of what he was saying. From the little bit I could make out, I thought he was asking if I wanted to go to Florida.

I pictured myself sunning by a hotel pool or taking a moonlit stroll on the beach with Tony. "Yes! I'd like to go on a vacation to Florida," I said.

"No," he whispered, "I mean for good—to coach the Bucs!"

"Tony, please don't play games with me," I said, sitting up. "It's cold outside. It's cold in the house, and I'm not in the mood." But he was so excited, and he doesn't get excited very often. He apologized for speaking so softly but told me he didn't want anyone else in the office to hear our conversation. I remember simply praying, *Please, God. I don't think I can handle another disappointment.*

After Tony's interview with Rich, Jerry Angelo, one of the Bucs' senior executives, had called Tony to set up a second interview. I didn't get my hopes up because Tony told me he couldn't figure out why they wanted to meet again. Steve Spurrier was surely going to take the job. "Maybe," he joked, "they just want to find out if I'm more coherent when I can see straight."

Now, a week after that second meeting, Jerry had called Tony, asking if he and I would fly down to Tampa to meet the team's owners.

"And, Lauren," Tony said, "they asked for my agent's number so they could start talking about a contract."

Later that evening, we discussed our prospects further. We tried to remain guarded after our disappointments with Philly and Jacksonville, thinking something could still go wrong. Tony cautioned me further, saying, "Jerry didn't say I had the job; he just said our visit and the contract negotiations need to go well." But then, we reasoned, why would the Bucs be asking me to come down with Tony and beginning to negotiate a contract if they weren't serious?

A couple of days later we landed at Tampa International Airport. The palm trees and sixty-five-degree temperature (about eighty-five degrees warmer than in Minneapolis) delighted our senses. I looked over at Tony and said, "Let's pray and ask God to *please* let this happen for us."

I did want to go back to Minnesota—but just long enough to scoop up Tiara, Jamie, and Eric. Otherwise, I was ready for Tampa!

Or so I thought. When we stepped off the plane, the chase was on. I had an idea then that we'd have to say good-bye to our quiet life outside the public eye. A mob of reporters chased us from the gate to the Airport Marriott, then down into the garage where Rich McKay was parked, waiting for us.

We raced off to dinner with the media in hot pursuit. Tony and I didn't know where we were going, just that we would be meeting the team's owners, the Glazer family, for dinner and that our meeting *had* to go well. But we knew nothing about the Glazers, and I wasn't sure what was going to take place. Would this be a formal interview where they would ask Tony questions? Would they ask me any questions? Did I need to make a good impression to help Tony secure the job? All these thoughts were racing through my mind as we pulled up to Bern's Steak House, an upscale restaurant that is a prime spot for business meetings—not only because of its excellent steaks and unique second-floor dessert room, but also because of its many private rooms.

I was relieved to discover that I wasn't the only woman there. Rich's wife, Terrin, met us. And Malcolm Glazer had brought his wife, Linda; their sons, Bryan and Joel; and their daughter, Darcie. The Glazers were very down-to-earth and engaging, and we had a wonderful time over dinner.

But as the evening progressed, I started to get a little concerned because there seemed to be very little discussion regarding football.

The restaurant had TV monitors, and we watched a live shot of the reporters who were gathered outside speculating: "Well, Tony Dungy must be signing the contract now." "They must be working out the final details."

From the inside, their comments were interesting—except we weren't signing a contract or working out details. As we were eating, we just talked about what a beautiful city Tampa is and how Tony and I could plug into the community.

I'm not sure what Tony was feeling, but the question I longed to ask was, *Do we have the job?*

TONY

The Glazers didn't officially offer me the coaching position over dinner. I knew they were still negotiating the finances with my agent, Ray Anderson. At this point, I didn't want anything to go wrong. So just as I hadn't asked Coach Noll the real question on my mind during our outing to Preservation Hall in New Orleans years before, I didn't ask where things stood that evening. As we wrapped up our meal, the reporters were still waiting out front, so I thought we'd go out the service entrance to avoid them.

Then Malcolm said, "Well, we should go down and introduce them to the new coach. Let's go out the front door." That's when we knew we were joining the Buccaneers. As we walked toward the door, I tried to take that thought in: *I am going to be the next head coach of the Bucs. Wow!* What a feeling that was.

The next day, I signed the contract at the Bucs' office. All the waiting and previous disappointments didn't matter now. My new job brought its own set of challenges, though. Once again, I would be separated from Lauren and our kids for a time. I settled for good in Tampa almost immediately, while Lauren headed back to Minnesota to prepare our house for the market.

I tease Lauren—a little—about how much different those last few months were in Minnesota. She actually liked the place. All of a sudden, being there without me in the winter wasn't so bad because she was preparing for our move to Florida. She even talked about doing some ice fishing on Lake Minnetonka!

Attitude shapes so many things, and Lauren's attitude toward Tampa was off the charts. It was going to be great no matter what because she was so excited to come. Lauren flew back and forth between the Twin Cities and Tampa quite a bit, trying to get established in our new city. One of the big challenges was figuring out where we were going to live because we weren't certain the team would be staying in Tampa. Hillsborough County had scheduled a vote that fall on a bond measure for a new stadium, and if it failed, the Glazers were going to move the team. Several such votes had failed previously. We heard all sorts of rumors about where the Bucs would go—Orlando, Cleveland, Los Angeles, or Hartford, Connecticut.

All the new coaches on our staff were afraid to buy houses, fearing we'd have to sell them in six months. So Lauren and I looked for a house to rent, rather than to buy. We also began searching for a church home—again. That was a big one. We had searched for so long in Minnesota, and now we were going to have to start the process all over.

In fact, our search would be even more complicated this time. We couldn't walk in and quietly observe a service. Everywhere we visited, people seemed to know who we were and went out of their way to make the new coach and his family feel welcome. But it made us uncomfortable. We just wanted to go in and worship, to get to know people and make friends normally. But that wasn't happening anymore. Lauren discovered that even when she would go by herself while I was on the road, people recognized her from the newspaper. She'd hear them whisper, "Why, it's the coach's wife!"

We settled in at First Baptist Church of College Hill, the church of Reverend Abe Brown. Reverend Brown had a tremendous impact on Lauren and me with his emphasis on being a light to the community. We both got involved with several of the church projects and also with Abe Brown Ministries, the prison outreach that Reverend Brown founded. Eventually, we ended up at Idlewild Baptist Church's central campus, which was also grounded in biblical preaching and offered phenomenal programs for our children.

Lauren

When Tony landed the job with the Bucs, I felt such a sense of accomplishment for him, as well as a sense that the Lord had orchestrated this. He had answered our prayers in His own timing. No one had predicted that Tony would get this job, and yet Mr. Glazer made clear he wanted him to join the Bucs.

When I flew back to Minnesota after the announcement, I was already thinking about how I could get involved and make an impact in Tampa. My goal was to include the wives in numerous events and functions, just as I'd seen done in Kansas City. I wanted to reach out and participate in community events, as well as help establish a family-oriented, positive culture for the team. As Tony began hiring coaches, I began talking with their wives from a distance, trying to help them get acclimated, even as I was learning my way around the city.

Relationships are so important to me. And being housebound so much of the year in Minnesota had been difficult. But that season of my life was behind me now. It was time to move forward and get involved in Tampa.

Still, I have to agree with Tony that attitude does make a difference because, all of a sudden, I didn't mind taking the dogs out for their walks in below-zero temperatures. Even though my to-do list was quite lengthy, I was energized by the projects I had to complete, such as finding new schools for the children. Tiara was in middle school, Jamie was in elementary school, and Eric was in preschool. I needed to be sure they finished that academic year strong while I investigated the schools in Tampa.

I also had to meet with the realtor and get our house in Minnesota listed. I had done it before, so it wasn't too overwhelming. In fact, nothing was going to steal my joy at that point. I didn't even mind the prospect of having to move twice once we settled in Tampa. I loved looking at the different kinds of architecture in Florida, and I thought renting might help us learn some things about the flavor and lifestyle of Florida living.

For instance, I wondered how families survived without a lower level or basement. Where did they store their extra belongings? Renting that first year was fine with me. I planned to be in Tampa for many years.

Before I knew it, the kids and I were in Tampa full time, enjoying our home with its palm trees in the front yard and fruit trees in the back. Of course, we could have rented almost anything in Tampa and it would have been fine with me.

I loved the home we had settled on, as well as the neighborhood. I thought it was wonderful to wake up, put on shorts and a sleeveless top, and go outdoors to bask in the Florida sunshine. I couldn't get over the sight of so many people outdoors all the time—swimming, biking, running, or dining on their porches in the beautiful tropical weather. Life was fabulous.

In fact, Tony still teases me about my response the first time we drove up to the Buccaneers' offices. "Oh, this is fantastic!" I said. I could see right away that the new offices were much smaller than those in the Vikings' complex. But what I couldn't tell was how worn and threadbare everything was. And I didn't notice the trailers that had been pieced together to make up part of the building.

Though it was obvious why the team needed to seek funding to build a new stadium, I never thought the Bucs would relocate. I had been praying for this move and felt it was God's plan for us to be in Tampa and to be used by Him there. There was constant speculation and discussion in the media, but none of it affected me. I was more concerned about something else I saw in the Tampa papers.

Every day the morning paper seemed to include an article on Tony, and sometimes it ran a feature story about our family.

With no games or even practices to write about, it was natural that the press would write about the new coach. They talked a lot about us, which was new for me. I wasn't accustomed to reading about what was going on in our personal lives. I often wondered where they got their information because initially I wasn't doing a lot of interviews. While Tiara wasn't overly thrilled to read about our family, Jamie welcomed the attention. He thought that it was cool to be included in the sports section, and he loved to call his friends back in Minnesota to tell them about it.

Eventually, I did do a couple of interviews, and my picture ran with the article. At the time, I was wearing my hair in long, distinctive braids. Perhaps that explains why so many people seemed to recognize me when I was out running errands or taking the kids places.

The people I met seemed sincerely interested in making us feel welcome, but it was difficult feeling as if they were watching *me*. It made me uncomfortable, and I was certain it wasn't good for our children. Tony was a little more used to it, and he kept reminding us that it goes with the territory. I didn't think I would ever get used to it.

Prayer really helped us through this time. We were going through so many changes and making so many decisions. We felt pulled in a thousand different directions. Tony and I were praying on the phone together during the day, and the kids and I would pray together in the evenings on the nights that Tony got home after they went to bed. If he was home, he would join us as well.

Praying together for wisdom and direction was so vitally important to staying grounded. Tony and I had been praying together since the beginning of our marriage, but sometimes not as consistently as we would have liked. Now we were doing it very regularly, both out of obedience to God and out of the awareness that our lives were so hectic and busy that we had to be extra careful not to slip. On top of that, we could not handle all our new responsibilities on our own.

Chapter 8

TAMPA'S TEAM

////////////////////

TONY

Creating time to pray together was the key for us as we made the move to Tampa. During difficult times, it's natural to pray more, asking God for help. But over the years we have seen that sometimes blessings can put a strain on a marriage. So we talked, walked, prayed, and tried to stay connected during our transition into a new city. That helped tremendously.

That's not to say the job ahead of me was an easy one. I may have achieved my goal of being named a head coach, but the team I was leading had been struggling for years. Part of the magnitude of the challenge came from the need to change the Bucs' culture. The Glazer family was new to owning a football team, and they wanted me to help integrate the team into the community in a positive way. That certainly fit with my idea for how a football team should operate—as an asset of the community at large—but it created additional stresses.

Lauren and I tried to work as a team to confront these challenges. I tackled many of the cultural issues within the organization—at least as they related to the business of football—such as how the coaches and players interacted with the community. Lauren had the opportunity to partner with me, and she jumped right in.

It's a good thing, because our lives had certainly gotten busier. Many of the opportunities were fantastic. For instance, we were able to go to the NFL owners' meetings, which were always held in vacation spots such as Phoenix or Palm Springs during the month of March. The owners, general managers, head coaches, and league officials get together there to vote on rule changes. I attended meetings much of the time, but for Lauren and the kids, it was in essence a vacation as they got to enjoy the setting. We also had fun participating with the Bucs in some of our city's traditions. For example, our entire family appeared with the team's float at the Gasparilla Parade of the Pirates, part of an annual festival that celebrates the legend of a mythical treasure-seeking pirate and his fellow buccaneers.

The opportunities to help in the community also became challenges because we were confronted with so many choices: luncheons, chances to meet with the media, public speaking engagements, and the like. All of these were terrific, but each would require more time away from home. Lauren and I realized that we had to be smart about which ones we would take on.

Even as we learned how to deal with more demands on our time, I was discovering that being a head coach didn't feel all that different from being a father. While I had more players than children to oversee—thankfully!—the principles were the same. I needed to champion values, talk about and model character and other positive traits, and make sure we were all doing what we needed to do. Whether I was on the field or in my home, I had to determine how I could best help each player or child. And I had learned from Coach Noll many years before that treating everyone fairly did not necessarily mean treating everyone the same. Different personalities required different types of encouragement and discipline.

In attempting to change the culture in Tampa Bay, we'd adopted a mantra: "No excuses; no explanations." The team members had spent so much time living in the past, captive to their circumstances and to other people's low expectations, that they needed to learn that we were not going to be victims any longer.

I'd borrowed Coach Noll's phrase, "Whatever it takes," so that the Bucs understood that because every game is different, no one could abdicate responsibility by saying, "That's not my job." We each had a contribution to make in building a winning team, and there would be times when we all would be asked to do a little more, depending on the circumstances.

Through it all, the Glazers demonstrated great confidence in me and our entire staff. They gave us a wide berth in trying to incorporate concepts from other teams we'd been a part of and create a team that did things the right way. Maximizing our talent and running the organization in the right way—focusing on the process—would bring wins in the long run.

Lauren
The owners' sons, particularly Joel and Bryan Glazer, wanted input from me and Tony on how to build a family-friendly

culture. They met with me often over informal business luncheons to ask for my thoughts. "What did you guys do in Minnesota with the wives?" was a typical question. I was eager to tell them how kickoff luncheons, parties, postgame events, and holiday parties were organized on other teams. I've always enjoyed entertaining and bringing people together, and we quickly developed a warm and productive relationship.

I also talked with the Glazers about how the team could help the families of new staff and players as they transitioned to Tampa. Once again, they were very receptive. Bryan gave me a team credit card so I could invite the new wives to lunch and answer their questions about everything from places to live, schools for their kids, churches where they could worship, to the best places to shop or get their hair done.

During games, I did my best to bring the wives and girlfriends of players and coaches together. During our first two years with the Bucs, the team played in the old Tampa Stadium—or the Big Sombrero as ESPN sportscaster Chris Berman affectionately called it. My "box" was a tiny cubbyhole. It was roomy enough for two metal folding chairs and a big old clunky tube TV, which interestingly enough was chained to a table. Even though there wasn't much room for entertaining, I was so happy to be in Florida that I didn't mind. I fondly remember how the TV would start flashing every time someone nearby flushed a commode.

When I told the Glazers about the game-day babysitting program that had been in place in Minnesota, they immediately embraced that idea. They provided the funding we needed to purchase toys and equipment, as well as to hire babysitters. That allowed the wives to enjoy the football games and support the team, knowing that their children were being cared for in a safe and secure room.

I also felt led to begin a pregame Bible study on Sundays for the families of players and coaches. The Glazers were willing to open up the stadium to accommodate this meeting. Christian motivational speakers ministered to the wives each week. They shared personal testimonies, prayed, and taught lessons. Many of the wives willingly shared how the Lord was working in their lives and ultimately encouraged one another through life challenges. One of the most impactful speakers was Veronica McGriff. Veronica grew up in Tampa and married her high school sweetheart, Fred McGriff, who went on to become a star baseball player with the Atlanta Braves before finishing his career with the Tampa Bay Rays. Veronica talked about being thrust into the limelight as Fred's career blossomed. She explained how she and Fred had to rely on the Lord to overcome the pitfalls that trapped so many of their peers. She was very transparent, and because she had already walked the path that many of our wives were just starting on, her story resonated with everyone. That was the kind of message I wanted to share with the wives to help them understand the dynamics of family life in the NFL and the importance of having a relationship with the Lord.

Another important part of my role was to increase the team's visibility within the community by representing the Buccaneer Women's Organization, which participated in charitable functions and community service projects throughout the Tampa Bay area. I told the Glazers about my desire to visit local schools to promote reading and help develop a love for literature in students, and they supported the launch of a literacy program. We invited players' and coaches' wives to accompany us, and those visits were a win-win situation. The wives were excited because they felt like they were using their gifts to help the kids in our community. The teachers were thrilled to have visitors to their classrooms who promoted reading. And it was great for the Bucs, too, because we always talked about the team when we reminded the students about the importance of reading. We explained that even players and coaches have to do homework to prepare for their games.

As the visibility of the women's organization increased, I began receiving more interview requests, along with invitations to speak at events or serve on various charitable boards. I wanted to let the community know what the Bucs and their women's organization were doing, so I welcomed the opportunities. At the same time, I had to learn to open up. Because I'd always been so private, that did not come naturally. It was one thing to interact with people one-on-one, but to stand up and be so transparent while presenting to a group wasn't something I was naturally comfortable with.

These invitations became a little overwhelming because I was also trying to plug the kids into life in Tampa. I didn't mind the constant pull myself, but I didn't want the kids to feel as if they were being thrust into the limelight. Our higher profile made me concerned about their security; at the same time, they needed to realize that everyone knew who we were. Their photos were everywhere—on television, in the paper, all over. We were just being cautious. We understood from the families of other head coaches that their children were picked on, and we were wary of that. Jamie, in particular, ended up taking criticism of Tony very personally.

In addition, while they had always been good kids, now they

had a new responsibility—to represent our family in public. That's something I wanted them to take seriously.

I realized I had to be careful myself whenever people would stop me and ask, "Hey, aren't you Mrs. Dungy? What do you think about Tampa?" Only months before I'd zip around town without anyone noticing; now, I constantly felt watched. I remember thinking, *I wonder if I have to dress a certain way. Do I have to put away my shorts and my casual clothes because people will be judging me? My hair—can I just put a baseball cap on, or do I have to maintain a certain image?*

I concluded that, no, I should just continue being the person that I am. My identity is in Christ, not in the world. And I didn't want the kids to think that Tony's new job would change who we were. It would be best to get to know people and for them to get to know us just as we were.

So in the end I didn't feel I had to conform to a certain image of the head coach's wife. If anything, with the Lord giving me a bigger and more visible platform, I needed to remain true to my core. I viewed my greater visibility as an opportunity to talk about the Lord and my faith. But I had to learn patience, too, and patience is not my strong suit. Many people assumed that if they weren't able to speak directly to Tony, then surely I would be glad to pass along a message for them.

I didn't really mind, but it was a little awkward when people at church, at the grocery store, or around town stopped me to ask if Tony could speak to their group. What made it especially hard was that the speaking requests were always for great causes, but Tony had limited time. Sometimes the person making the request would say, "If he could only come once, for just a few minutes . . ." Given the sheer volume of requests, however, we'd never have had any family time if he'd accepted very many of them.

One reason I enjoyed my work with the Bucs was that it gave me and Tony a sense that we were accomplishing something important together. Even though Tony had more responsibilities and was busier than ever, it didn't seem like it because we shared common goals.

I spent a lot of time at One Buc. Many days I drove to the team's offices, and I would always see Tony or pop my head in his office to say hello. Sometimes he'd be busy and we wouldn't be able to talk long, but I felt very involved in what he was doing. It wasn't a situation where he disappeared at dawn and came back late at night.

Still, with all that was going on, it was important for Tony and me to stay connected. It was harder now, but we recognized that we had to make a conscious effort to keep our quality time as the pace of life picked up.

TONY

Lauren and I were able to talk a lot during the day. As she mentioned, sometimes we were able to talk at the office, but I'd also learned from watching her on the phone with her mom that she is very relational. I made it a point to call between meetings just to say hi and check in for a couple of minutes whenever I could.

We continued taking evening walks as well. We lived in a quiet neighborhood on a golf course, and we could walk on the course anytime without interruption. Nobody was going to stop us or sit down with us and start a conversation.

To ensure that all my players and staff were able to have meaningful downtime with their families during the season,

I followed Denny Green's schedule from Minnesota and kept Friday afternoons free from work activities. The team would have a short practice that ended about 12:45. Afterward we'd have a family cookout. The rest of the day was open so that families could spend time together.

On most Friday afternoons, Lauren and I did something with the kids. Many times we let them choose the activity, whether it was a trip to Chuck E. Cheese's, the park, or a movie. Often, Lauren and I would designate that evening as our date night. We thought it was so important to build in time for each other, especially with such a busy lifestyle. Date nights gave us time to catch up and enjoy each other without interruption.

Lauren and I also knew it was important to keep tabs on our kids to see how they were handling the transition to Tampa. They had loved living in Minnesota, so even though the new job was good news, they had been sad to leave their friends and their cousins. We continued holding family meetings around the dinner table as a way to stay connected with them. We knew our life now was very similar to living in a fishbowl. Being the head coach's kids had its perks and its pressures. Lauren and I knew we had to be intentional about keeping our family together, balanced, and on board, as well as to know what our kids were experiencing—both good and bad.

Since I wanted some one-on-one time with the kids, we decided I would drive them to school each morning. I couldn't always control when my workday would end, but I could spend thirty to forty minutes in the car with them before heading to the office. We had a long drive to their schools, so it turned out to be a great time to connect. Eric used to call in to Joy FM, the Christian radio station in Tampa, and request "The Cartoon

Song" by Chris Rice *every day*. It got to be a running joke. The DJ would say, "It's 7:20, and we've got Eric from Tampa on the line. . . ."

Lauren picked up the kids in the afternoons. She would tell me that from the moment Eric got in the car, he talked nonstop. He loved his kindergarten class at Berkeley Prep and wanted to share details of the entire day with us. Lauren learned to suggest the kids play the "quiet game" for five minutes just so Tiara and Jamie would have a chance to jump in. They all joked that Eric definitely took after the Harrises with his gift of gab!

Prioritizing family time was something Lauren and I learned from Coach Noll when we first got married. He gave his assistant coaches plenty of vacation time and always scheduled a long break before training camp began. He took those breaks himself, and he never called us over the summer asking us to come into the office or to work on a special project. In fact, from the time we broke until we were scheduled to come back, we never heard from him. For the first eight years of our marriage, Lauren and I knew we had the month of June and the first part of July to ourselves, and we loved it. That was our time to reconnect and do things we enjoyed as a family.

Not everybody I worked with after that saw family time as important, but when I became the boss and could set the schedule, I followed Coach Noll's example. I knew how much those breaks helped our marriage, and I wanted my coaches to benefit from them too. A long season puts a strain on the family, and I wanted families as healthy as possible before the stresses of another season hit.

Our extended families continued to play an important part in our lives when we moved to Tampa. In fact, relatives from both sides of our family began visiting more often. The Florida sunshine was a big attraction—especially in the winter. As always, my parents liked to set their own schedule when they visited, and Tiara, Jamie, and Eric loved spending time with them, whether hanging out at the mall or watching late-night sports coverage on TV.

My parents' plans didn't always mesh well with the homework and bedtime routines that Lauren had established for the kids, but she learned to roll with that when they were in town. While Lauren preferred things structured, she saw how much love the kids were getting from their grandparents. We didn't let them stay up all night, but they could enjoy some time with Gram and Grandad. Because Lauren chose relationships over structure, the memories the older kids have of their grandparents are priceless.

Shortly after moving to Tampa, we encountered a bigger, much longer-lasting stressor: building our house. It was something we'd looked forward to, but the building process seemed to go on forever.

In September 1996, area residents voted on whether to approve funding for the new stadium. While the votes were being counted, I was at work. Supposedly I was getting ready for the Detroit Lions, but actually I was keeping more of an eye on the TV coverage. The numbers kept changing, and it was so close that following the count was nerve-racking. I watched nervously as the tallies went from 49 percent in favor to 50.3 percent to 49.8 percent to 51 percent and finally . . . victory! The team would be staying in Tampa.

Now Lauren and I knew we could start building our dream house. In Minnesota, the builder had been able to guarantee that our home there would be completed in four months. So I was a little surprised when our Florida builder told us it would probably take six to nine months. When I asked for that in writing, it became twelve months. In the end, it actually took much longer—almost nineteen months.

Though they were far away, Lauren's family offered their help with the house. Lauren's brother Loren was the most involved. He wanted to be sure we were getting our money's worth every step of the way and knew I didn't have a lot of time to research and check up on the builder. He would make periodic visits to check on the progress—shake the windows, peel back insulation, and give his opinion on the workmanship, either to us, or if he was around, to the builder.

I noticed that most of his visits happened to coincide with Bucs home games and teased him about that. As much as he loved coming to the games, though, I knew Loren wanted us to end up with a comfortable home, and I appreciated that.

Nonetheless, as anyone who has ever had a house built knows, the delays and cost overruns can make homeowners a little crazy. Lauren and I did have some arguments, mainly over little things, but sometimes a breakdown in communication would lead to conflict. Whose fault was it? Had I misinterpreted what Lauren wanted, or had we not communicated our preference to the builder correctly? Maybe she didn't spell it out just right, or maybe she'd been clear and the builder had made a mistake.

During this time, we were reminded that sometimes it's best to apologize even when you don't think you caused the disagreement. When that happened, one of us would choose to say, "I love you. Now let's move forward." That's not easy to do,

Our dating days . . .

. . . and our wedding day:
June 19, 1982

Heading to the airport in style after our wedding reception

Casey the "German shepherd"? (LEFT)

Corey: The German shepherd we added to our family after it turned out Casey wasn't one at all! (BELOW LEFT)

Our first family photo with Tiara (ABOVE)

Fun with Tiara and Jamie at a Steelers game day program (LEFT)

Arriving in Tampa in 1996. We couldn't believe our rental house had a pool! (TOP: *Lauren, Eric, Tony;* BOTTOM: *Tiara, Jamie*) (ABOVE)

Hanging out with Loren, Lauren's twin brother, in Pittsburgh (ABOVE)

On the Bucs float at Tampa's Gasparilla Parade, 1997 (L TO R: *Tony, Eric, Jamie, Lauren, Tiara*) (RIGHT)

The Colts' AFC Championship victory in 2007. After an incredible journey, we were finally on our way to the Super Bowl!

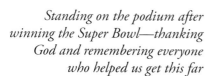

Standing on the podium after winning the Super Bowl—thanking God and remembering everyone who helped us get this far

At the White House after winning the Super Bowl

Having fun at Yellowstone on a camping trip with the Morans, Gordons, and Dr. and Mrs. Ben Carson (LEFT)

All dressed up for a Family First banquet (RIGHT)

With Jordan and Eric on the field at Plant High School Senior Night (November 2009)

*Our 2009 family Christmas card picture. (*TOP: *Eric, Lauren [holding Jason], Tony [holding Justin];* BOTTOM: *Tiara, Jade, Jordan)*

Jason's adoption in 2010
(LEFT)

Jason got to meet President Obama and Vice President Biden at a Town Hall meeting at the University of Tampa! (BELOW)

Our first trip as a family to Oregon, where Eric would be playing for the Ducks. Here we are with "Puddles" at the spring game in 2010. (LEFT)

Bowling with Mike and Barb Cephas: our kids' godparents and our dear friends

Reading from the first children's book we wrote together: You Can Be a Friend *(2011)*

Visiting Tampa elementary schools to support reading programs . . . (ABOVE)

. . . and this time, Jade had the day off school and came with us! (RIGHT)

Looking ahead and hoping God grants us thirty more wonderful years together

especially when emotions have gotten heated. It goes against our human nature, but it works when minor disagreements crop up.

In any event, we didn't want to let those issues divide us. We were enjoying everything else so much. We had rented a house right around the corner from where we were building, so the kids were getting to know their neighborhood, and they weren't going to have to change schools.

Although I sometimes felt as if the construction of our new home was out of my hands, I remained absolutely committed to my plan to build a winning football team. Early on, though, I wasn't sure which would be accomplished first. By the end of September, we had a 0–5 record. After that fifth loss we had a bye week, and Bryan and Joel Glazer asked me to go to lunch with them. They told me that while they were disappointed in our start, they wanted me to know that they were with me for the long haul. I really appreciated that. I was also encouraged by something Coach Noll would say whenever I asked him for advice: "Don't change what you believe in." I knew how his own team had struggled his first two seasons before things began to click. "Stick with what you believe in, even though it's not always going to be popular." And so I did, and Lauren was there to support me in that.

After my lunch with the Glazers, our team started to play better, but it didn't show up on the scoreboard. Our record fell to 1–8, and the fans who had had such high expectations were very disappointed. Six months earlier, people had been excited to welcome us to Tampa, but the honeymoon was definitely over. It was tough on our family, especially the kids, to leave the stadium and hear the disgruntled voices of our fans. I think Lauren could sense my frustration when I came home as well.

We hadn't been expecting this. When we came to Tampa, everything had been so perfect that we felt sure we would begin winning pretty quickly.

But we persevered as a family, and the team finished that first season on a high note, winning five of our last seven games. Then, early in the next season, things began to gel on the field. I had laid out the ground rules and expectations the first year, and now our players seemed to know what they had to do. During our first year, let's just say tickets had not been hard to get. But when we opened the second year with five straight wins, games started selling out and the atmosphere in the stadium became electric.

Lauren

In 1997, I noticed a big difference off the field as well as on it. When people talked to me, they started to refer to the team as "we," whereas the year before it had always been "the Bucs" or "your husband's team." The community was starting to identify with the team, and you could feel that connection everywhere you went in town. Many local organizations also requested that the Buccaneer Women's Organization assist them through fashion shows, TV appearances, interviews, and hospital visits. It was an exciting time.

Our second season in Tampa was special for me in another way. That's the year the Bucs drafted Warrick Dunn from Florida State. Though he was only twenty-one, he had responsibility for three teenage children—his siblings. Warrick had been raised by his mom and grandmother in Baton Rouge. His mom was a police officer and a single parent. Warrick, the oldest child, was always the man of the house.

Then, during Warrick's senior year of high school, his mom had been tragically killed during an attempted armed robbery at a bank. Before her death, he'd promised to be there for his brothers and sisters. During his first year with us, Warrick's grandmother kept his siblings at their home in Baton Rouge, and he stayed in constant communication with her.

The following year, however, he determined that it would be best to move his siblings to Tampa to live with him. So here was this young, soft-spoken recent college graduate who was launching a pro football career while also raising children on his own. It was all new for him. He knew the Bucs had high expectations for him on the team, but he thought it was equally important to raise his family the right way.

That gave me a wonderful opportunity to help in small ways. I used to go with him to parent-teacher meetings, just to provide another listening ear. Sometimes Warrick would call and ask, "Can I bounce something off you? What do you think about that? This isn't working; what do you suggest?"

Before long, Warrick and I spoke about once a week. During the school year, I think he was reassured knowing someone would go with him to meetings with the teachers. He wanted to stay on top of the kids and their progress in school. He told me, "Everyone sees me on the field and thinks of me as a great athlete, but I also love my brothers and sisters. I want to be there for them and help them navigate through those teenage years. I want to emphasize how important it is to do well in school and succeed, not just ride on my coattails."

I thought he was so mature and wise beyond his years. In light of his popularity, he never lost sight of his goal to provide a stable home for his brothers and sisters. He didn't want people hanging around just because of his fame. If they could help his brothers and sisters be better students and succeed in the way he knew his mother wanted, then he was open. Otherwise, he wasn't interested.

Warrick wasn't the only player whom Tony and I reached out to. As we got to know the players better, we became more like a family to them. We often heard about their issues and problems. We thought it a privilege to be able to pray with players and their families or to simply sit and talk with them. We knew our limits, though, and sometimes encouraged them to get professional help. If they needed someone to watch their kids while they sought counseling, we'd do it.

We did our best to model a healthy marital relationship to the entire team. The Glazers took their family on team trips, and they encouraged us to do the same. During our second year, Jamie began going with us to the away games while a babysitter stayed at home with Tiara and Eric. Once he got a little older, Eric came with us as well. Our boys always looked forward to those trips. In order to come with us, however, we required that they do well in school the week before.

As we operated as a team in front of the players and our own kids, we learned that operating as a unit didn't mean we had to let tradition define who did what in our household. I dislike using the words *strengths* and *weaknesses*, but there are some things that Tony is more gifted at doing and others that I feel I am better equipped to do. The key is working together to ensure we're each handling those things we do best.

It's a pretty simple concept, but not everyone understands the principle. Rather than holding on to rigid, defined roles of "the husband does this; the wife does that," we have learned to work together as a unit so the family will function best.

So if I end up fixing things around the house because Tony is on a road trip, that's okay. And if it works out better for him to drive the kids to school in the morning, he does it. He's never asked, "What would it look like to have an NFL head coach sitting in the car-pool line?" And I appreciate that.

The other side of it is recognizing the areas where we or our spouses are not as gifted. As I was growing up, my parents ran a tight ship. They had a lot to manage: not only did they have a lot of children, but my dad was an entrepreneur who juggled multiple responsibilities. My mom kept everything organized, a trait I admired and try to emulate.

If I could, I'd wave a magic wand and we Dungys would all be that way. Guess what? Tony's not an overly neat person, so even today keeping our home in order falls to me. I'm constantly going to the store to buy crates, file folders, and boxes. Everything runs so much more smoothly in an orderly household. I have little cubbies in the laundry room where our kids put their things. I do a lot of color-coding to keep items organized too. I have my master calendar in the kitchen—a big paper one, not something digital on a phone. Though Tony is not as concerned about such things, I think he recognizes how much better everyone functions when there's order and less confusion in the household.

Tony tells me I shouldn't be surprised by his messiness since I saw what his dad's study looked like the very first time we visited his parents' house. I wonder if perhaps he should just acknowledge that he's a chip off the old block!

It's too bad that Tony's office is just inside the front door. It's the first room people see when they come into our house. With all his helmets, pictures, mementos, and awards, it could be a showplace. When *Ebony* magazine wanted to do a photo shoot there, I hired someone to come in and fix it up. They organized everything and put up pictures and plaques on the wall. It was beautiful. Then, after the shoot, things began piling right back up again.

I cringe whenever I hear Tony tell someone, "Well, come into my office so I can show you. . . ." I'm thinking, *I would be so embarrassed.* But he's okay with it. On the other hand, I'm afraid to take anyone in there; they might not be able to find their way back out!

Still, I just close the door. I've learned to accept it and let it go. You have to pick your battles, and worrying about Tony having a clean and orderly study is not going to be one of mine.

On the other hand, because I keep the house organized, Tony can concentrate more on the bookkeeping. That's where he excels. I know enough that I can be involved with it, even though he writes the checks and pays the bills. We've come to understand each other's strengths, and we each recognize that the other person might be better equipped to handle a particular task.

I think anytime a couple models what a good marriage looks like, it speaks volumes to others. When Tony was a head coach, we thought it was important, especially for the younger players, to see the stability between us and the fact that, no matter the outcome of the game, we, as a couple, were in it together.

Chapter 9

LIVING THE DREAM

///////////////////

TONY

By our second season in Tampa, everything was on the upswing, and everything we'd dreamed about seemed to be happening. Our kids were thriving, the Bucs were building a winning team, and we and the team were involved in community activities. Lauren had started volunteering at First Baptist in the church food pantry, and I would join her when I had a free lunch hour. Reverend Abe Brown had taken me on a prison visitation, and I'd fallen in love with that outreach. Lauren started going on some of those trips as well, and it reinforced the importance of family for us even more. As we talked with young inmates, we could see that many of their problems stemmed from unstable home lives.

I had also started working with an organization called Family First. Together with Mark Merrill, its founder and president, we launched a fatherhood program called All Pro Dad. The Bucs hosted a huge event for the Big Brothers Big Sisters program, and four or five of our players had signed up to be Big Brothers. That was exactly the kind of buy-in to the community that I'd had in mind when we came to Tampa.

Once the team started winning, we almost felt like the first family of our city. The boys loved the spotlight and spent as much time with the team as possible. Jamie had become a regular visitor to my office in Minnesota, so hanging out at the Bucs' complex felt pretty normal to him. With his dad in charge, though, he pretty much had free rein. And he enjoyed that. Now five-year-old Eric joined him, and he could be a handful. From the time he was little, he was into football and all over the place.

Tiara wasn't at the office as much as the boys because she was often busy with her own activities after school. Cross country was her favorite sport, so many of her fall afternoons were spent running with her teammates. And while she didn't necessarily like the football spotlight and preferred shopping trips with Lauren to being at One Buc, she did enjoy coming to the complex for our family cookouts.

During training camp at the University of Tampa, my boys worked as ball boys. They stayed with me in my training-camp dorm room until school started. One of the first times Eric was there, he was run over by a golf cart driven by one of our trainers. Eric shed quite a few tears, but once he calmed down and we realized he was fine, it was actually pretty funny. That staff member was so afraid he would be fired for hurting the coach's son! After that I kept a better eye on Eric, but it didn't take long for everyone to get used to having Jamie and Eric around.

On Saturday mornings during the season, the boys expected to pack up and go to work with me. On most weekday afternoons during the school year, Lauren dropped them off at the Bucs complex after picking them up from school. However, they knew coming down wasn't a right; it was an incentive if they finished their homework early or did well in a class.

Darin Kerns was the Bucs' equipment manager, and he loved those boys. He told me to bring them back to him anytime I wanted, and he would put them to work. They loved helping him because he had TVs and video games in his area. Whenever Jamie and Eric got bored somewhere else, that's where they'd go. They knew their territory in the building, and they knew where they were allowed to go on the field.

In addition to the equipment area, the boys loved going to the cafeteria, where they found they could get treats whenever they wanted. Jose Garcia was the team chef, and he always took care of the coaches' kids. They snacked on bowls of cereal, cookies, or ice cream, which were available any time of day.

One of Jamie's biggest thrills happened during the playoff game against the Detroit Lions on December 28, 1997—the Bucs' first home playoff game in eighteen years. Jamie had done well in school, so as a reward, I let him hold my headset cord during the game. Coaches' headsets were not yet wireless, so Jamie's job was to manage the slack in the cord as I moved up and down the sideline. Fox TV announcer John Madden pointed Jamie out during the broadcast, actually circling him on the Telestrator during the game.

When he got to school the next day, Jamie was a hero! It seemed as if everyone in Tampa—including all of his classmates—had watched us defeat the Lions. The newspaper did a story on Jamie and pointed out that the Bucs had never lost a game when Jamie was holding his dad's cord. The fans were calling in to talk shows to say that I *had* to take Jamie to Green Bay for the next playoff game. So Lauren and I told Jamie that if he did well in school that week, he could make his first road trip. Of course, we had no problems getting him to do his homework that week!

I remember watching Darin get Jamie all bundled up in the locker room to go out for the warm-ups. The next thing I knew, Jamie, who looked like a big snowman, was out on the field shaking hands with Packers quarterback Brett Favre. We lost that playoff game to Green Bay, but it didn't put much of a damper on the season. When we flew back home after the game, a huge crowd was waiting at our offices. They cheered for every single person as we got off the buses. Reggie Roberts, our public relations director, had to get security to help us through the crowd and to our car. I couldn't imagine what it would have been like if we had won the game!

Not everyone in our family, however, thought being part of the coach's family was ideal. In fact, my position as head coach with the Bucs came with some costs. It was a little harder to simply be yourself, especially for the kids. It was harder to go out together or for them to be out with me.

Tiara talked about that all the time. If we were going to the mall, she would say, "Why can't Mom just take me?" When we lived in Minnesota, she sometimes said that—but then it was probably because I was wearing brown pants with an orange shirt and she thought I looked like a nerd. That didn't bother me, but now I knew she didn't want to go out with me because there was a good chance we'd get stopped by a fan wanting to talk.

It hurt to know that Tiara didn't want to be with her dad in public. Lauren and I tried to explain that the loss of some privacy goes with the territory. We pointed out the many benefits that went along with my job—a comfortable house, nice vacations, and perks from the team. Even so, I understood where she was coming from. She was adamant that people like her because she was Tiara, not because she was a Dungy. In fact, when she got a job at Publix, the manager told her that it was store policy that she include a last name on her name tag. So she did—hers read "Tiara Lee," with the fictitious surname she had added for herself.

Lauren

That loss of privacy can be particularly tough when the team loses. It was such a disappointment, knowing all the time and effort that went into preparing for the game. The hardest defeats of all were the heartbreakers that were lost in the final seconds. Yet even after those games, I knew Tony would be up bright and early the next day, ready to go to work to assess what happened—what the team did right, what they did wrong, what they needed to correct.

It always seemed like such a long week after a loss. Friends and family wanted to know what happened. I would explain that I didn't have the answers. I wasn't the coach, but I came to realize that when people couldn't ask Tony, they would ask me. That was part of the job. So I developed my "Tony" answers—all the things I would hear him say: "We're just going to have to play harder and a little smarter next time. We made too many mistakes, but the coaches and players will get them corrected at practice." I learned to stay upbeat because people were watching—they were even watching me.

Because of our prominence in the community, invitations to events began pouring in as well. It was challenging, particularly at first, to discern what to say yes to and what to pass on. Early on, I think I realized I needed to be careful about my soft heart. If an opportunity revolved around children or helping families in need, I was always tempted to get involved. Yet I needed to be concerned about our own family too.

Many events for great causes were on the weekends of home games when our kids also had activities. Our family, we agreed, had to come before outside causes. Our children's sports and other activities were just as important as anything else we were doing. Juggling their schedules alone was hard, so we really had to be careful not to take on too much more.

These outside opportunities reminded us how important communication was. Tony wanted to know which causes I felt strongly about supporting, but he also was open to hearing when I felt we needed to cut back on our commitments. He knew I was aware of how our schedules were impacting the kids.

As the number of requests increased, we realized how important it is to be discerning because the good can quickly become the enemy of the best. We discovered that it can be hard to understand what the Lord wants in your life. He brings many opportunities, but we have to decide which ones will be most significant, what will most benefit the Kingdom of God, and what the costs will be. Tony and I talked a lot about maintaining our priorities—God, each other, our children, and then other important causes.

We certainly wanted to give back to the community, but we quickly realized that every free moment would be taken if we weren't careful. We—and especially me—had to learn how to say no to very worthwhile causes. Often those making the requests had difficulty understanding why we had to say no. Many would say, "But it's just a phone call" or "Couldn't you stop by our event for just thirty minutes?"

Tony's assistant, Lora McCarthy, became our first line of defense. Whenever someone would start telling me about something he or she wanted Tony and me to do, I'd say, "Send it to Lora. She knows Tony's schedule." Lora would investigate the person and organization making the request to find out exactly what the commitment was and what the purpose of the event was. She would take each letter and either highlight the key details or write little notes to help us quickly sort through what the person was asking and what the commitment really entailed. Tony would bring the letters home in a folder and place them on the dining room table until we had time to go through them.

From the beginning, Lora was good at knowing our hearts and what we might want to support. She probably declined about 80 percent of the requests up front, usually because she knew they wouldn't work with our schedule or because she knew they didn't align with the causes closest to our hearts. We carefully considered the requests she did pass on to us.

The whole process was a great exercise. It made us carefully examine what our passion was and what was in our hearts—what we really wanted to do and what we felt fit within our God-ordained priorities. For instance, we decided early on that we wouldn't sit on any boards. If we were going to take time away from our family, we wanted to do something hands-on. We also started to involve our kids. Whenever possible, we took them with us—especially for hospital visits or children's programs. We wanted them to see what we were doing and to learn about helping others and giving back. But no matter how much we prayed and thought about the opportunities, it was hard disappointing people who had poured their hearts into causes that meant so much to them.

Tony and I often came back to some great advice that Tom Lamphere had given Tony when he was coaching in Minnesota. He said there are plenty of things Tony could do to help people, but many of those things other people could do too. Tony needed to look for the things other people couldn't do as well as he could. If someone else could do it well, then Tony wouldn't be maximizing his gifts or his time. Since then we've kept that counsel in mind as we weigh ministry or speaking opportunities. Is it something we really want to do? Could the organizers get someone else to do it? Is there something unique we can add, whether visibility or an ability we have that others don't?

TONY

Things were moving right along in Tampa. The 1997 season had ended with a playoff loss, but we'd moved into the new stadium and had a playoff appearance under our belt—everything felt so great.

By 1998, however, the bloom was off the rose. Things didn't pan out as we'd planned, and we learned on the final day of the season that we hadn't made the playoffs. While disappointing, we still loved Tampa, and we felt as if the community loved us in return.

The next year, 1999, was a better year for our football team. We started off inconsistently; in fact, we fell to 3–4 after seven games. Without any major changes in personnel or philosophy, we suddenly got hot at midseason. By just being a little more tuned in to the details, we got on a six-game winning streak and put ourselves in first place in our division.

Along with playing better on the field, our players were also active in the community, using their platform for good at schools and during other appearances. More of our games were being nationally televised during prime time, and all of this meant the Bucs were receiving much more exposure than they had in earlier years.

We finished the regular season with eleven wins, the most in team history, and we were back in the playoffs. We beat the Washington Redskins in our first playoff game, but the following week we came up just short in the NFC Championship game, losing to the St. Louis Rams, 11–6.

Having such a great year and getting so close to a Super Bowl appearance should have had everyone excited and looking forward to the 2000 season. However, right after the loss to the Rams, the Glazers came to me with a request that really shook me up. In the past, they had been so supportive of all my football decisions, but they were now expressing some concern. Unhappy that we hadn't scored many points in our two playoff games, they wanted me to fire our offensive coordinator, Mike Shula. I didn't think that was the right thing to do, and for about two weeks I wrestled with whether I should take a stand on behalf of my staff member or go along with the wishes of my bosses. I talked to Lauren quite a bit, as well as to several of the pastors and chaplains who had given me spiritual guidance over the years.

After a lot of thought and prayer, I decided to respect the authority of my bosses and fire Mike. Almost immediately, though, I regretted doing so. Bryan and Joel's decision to get involved in football matters undercut our team's family atmosphere and ultimately portended things to come, even if we didn't see it at the time.

While Mike's termination in February 2000 would change the dynamics on our staff, Joe Marciano, another one of my coaches, had recently done something that would lead to major changes in our family's life. Joe had joined my coaching staff when we came to Tampa in 1996. He was single but loved kids and wanted to adopt a son. Even though he knew what the challenges would be, he was committed to being a full-time dad as well as a full-time coach. He just needed a little help from me to enable him to do that. Because he was the special teams coach, I realized he didn't have to meet with the other coaches. Instead, he and I worked out a time when the two of us could meet to review his plans for the kicking game. Of course, once Joe's son, Joseph, arrived, Lauren and the other coaches' wives rallied around them too.

Not long after, Lauren and I began discussing the possibility of adding to our family by adopting. Or I should say that's when Lauren started discussing it with me. She told me she felt as if the Lord was speaking to her, saying that in this season of our lives, maybe we needed to adopt a child. He was telling her, *You have the resources. You have the home and the loving family.* Yet she was careful to tell me she wanted to be sure she wasn't being driven by her own desire but by the Lord's leading. She was aware that I wasn't feeling the same pull that she was—at least not as strongly.

Though it was a serious topic, I joked with her. "No, I can't say I've heard the Lord on this point. But then again I am turning forty-five. Maybe my hearing is going?"

We agreed to pray about it to make sure the Lord was speaking to both of us. We wanted to know, "Is this a pull that's going to pass, or is this really the Lord speaking?" Of course, that's always the question when a couple is confronted with a major decision that will dramatically change their lives. How do you know when God is speaking to you? We've always tried to come to peace about a decision and be sure we are on the same page.

I had concerns about adopting an infant, but I was open to investigating it with Lauren. I knew how much she loves kids, and I knew watching Joe welcome a baby into our team family had kindled that desire in her. I was about to turn forty-five, though, and wondered if I would have the time or the energy to parent another baby. I just wasn't sure whether it was the right time for us to adopt.

Then Lauren asked me when it would ever be "the right time." We could always point to something else that was keeping us busy. Yet she made very clear that she knew this had to be our decision. If we didn't agree that we should proceed, it might be the Lord's way of telling us that it wasn't the right time, even though adoption sounded like a wonderful idea. We tell other couples that it's not wise to adopt because you think it will help your marriage. Adopting never fixes something that's broken or resolves other issues families are struggling with.

Still, as Lauren's husband, I knew I needed to be biblical and love my wife sacrificially, as it says in Ephesians 5. The Bible's number one instruction to a husband is to love his wife. And that means working hard to hear her heart on issues and then striving to meet her needs.

Sometimes for a man to love his spouse, he must put her feelings first. I had to remind myself that being "head of the household" didn't mean I had to make all the decisions for our family. Hopefully, we agree on major decisions. That's the goal, but it doesn't always happen—as with my decision to leave Kansas City for Minnesota. But I have learned that when making those big decisions, I have to know my wife's heart and I have to listen to the Lord.

Once I understood Lauren's passion for adoption and the "rightness" of it in God's eyes, Lauren and I talked about its effects on our family and agreed we could do it together. In the end, we both had peace of mind about it.

Even so, we had slightly different ideas about how to proceed. My big question became, "What's the best way to do this?" I was more concerned about the process than Lauren was. I think she was a little frustrated with me as I tried to talk through everything. She said, "Well, let's use the same people Joe used and get moving."

This reminded us that the Lord often brings together different people to complement each other. I'm very much like my dad. I tend to proceed slowly and analyze a situation before making a big decision, while Lauren gathers her information and then, boom, she's ready to act.

I knew that it had taken Joe about eighteen months to complete his adoption, so I figured we had time to prepare to bring a new child into our family; if anything, I feared having to navigate a lot of red tape. What I found out when we actually sat down with the woman from the adoption agency convicted me that God truly was in our decision to adopt. Although I'd been concerned about delays, she told us that there was a real shortage of African American adoptive parents. If we were considering an African American or biracial child, she had several to choose from *immediately*. And if we wanted a newborn, she felt that could happen quickly as well because she didn't have any African Americans on her waiting list. That was convicting to me, and it convinced me that this was the "right time" for us.

Lauren

A married couple needs to focus on both partners' passions and desires. Otherwise, one of the spouses may be forgotten. It can be so easy to forget that what is important to one partner might not be as important to the other.

I had always been supportive of Tony's career in sports. We sacrificed, made adjustments, and moved around the country because that was what needed to happen. He was passionate about his job, and I loved supporting him. I think Tony felt the same way about my desire to adopt at that point in our lives. He might not have been as excited about it as I was, but he recognized the importance of what I was experiencing. I believe the Lord speaks to us in many different ways: through the Bible, prayers, and the counsel of other people. I was getting information on adoption from a lot of sources, and I didn't feel it was a coincidence. I found myself praying about it more and more, and I definitely felt that God was trying to get my attention.

I think watching my parents and grandparents adopt later in their lives made the decision a very natural and comfortable one for me. I never doubted that we would we be able to love and support a child in this season of our lives.

Tony and I brought Jordan home in August 2000. And right away we had to deal with something we hadn't experienced with our other children—colic. We were still able to take our regular walks; we just pushed our son in his stroller as he cried. As we walked the neighborhood in the dark with Jordan, I'm sure the neighbors wondered, *Why are the Dungys pushing a crying baby in a stroller in the middle of the night?* Those early days were a little stressful, but we made it work, and the colic didn't last forever.

The older kids were so helpful and quickly bonded with the baby. Tiara, in particular, loved having a baby brother. We hadn't talked about our decision to adopt with the children until we had decided on it as a couple, and then we presented it to them as a final decision. They were good with it. After we had Jordan at home, Tiara would often say, "I think I need to stay home from school to help out or go with you to the doctor's appointment." We didn't let her, but she and the boys loved having Jordan in the family. There was no jealousy or resentment, just a lot of love and happiness with the new addition.

Yet soon we realized that colic was the least of our concerns. Jordan cried when he was hungry, but that was it. He didn't cry when he got his immunizations. He didn't cry when he fell off a bed. His teeth came in very early, and soon I started to find them in his crib or on the floor. I panicked. At first I thought they were coming in too soon and just not holding, but then we saw him pulling them out!

We found out that such problems had been evident shortly after birth. We were told he hadn't cried in the hospital during his circumcision or when he was given eyedrops. So it was obvious something was different with him, but no one knew what it was. In our anxious moments, we had to come back to trusting the Lord to lead us to the right people.

This was a new challenge for us. Our first three children had no real health issues. Jamie experienced two seizures when he was small. Although they were scary, once he was put on the proper medication, he never had any more problems. But with Jordan we could tell something wasn't quite right. And once we began consulting the doctors, we realized we were in for some long-term issues. We knew we owed it to Jordan to do all we could to give him the best care and to figure out what was going on.

Jordan's health problems had the potential to disrupt our marriage. We had to consult with many doctors because of his rare condition while also making time for ourselves, limited as it was. We kept getting more referrals to specialists, first in Tampa, then at the University of Florida, and finally at Johns Hopkins in Baltimore. None of the doctors in Florida had seen anything like this.

This was another time in our marriage when our personality differences became very evident. I'm more emotional, so I was upset by each recommendation that we see another specialist. Tony is a little more laid-back. He receives information quietly. It was great to have that balance because I was ready to fall apart whenever I received difficult news, but Tony was able to take in and process the information to help us move forward.

The flip side was that occasionally I wanted to see more passion from Tony. Jordan's needs were unique and not well understood, even by most of his doctors. A number of health issues might have been overlooked or not addressed if I hadn't challenged some of the doctors and specialists. Through this experience, I realized that I saw the long-term consequences of the doctors' decisions on Jordan and tended to be more directly affected by them than Tony was, simply because I spent more time with our son.

Together we were Jordan's advocates and his voice. We had to be willing to fight for him. When I felt Tony was a little too laid-back, I would treat the problem more aggressively. I wanted to jump on it and make those phone calls and schedule those appointments right away. I knew, though, that it wasn't that Tony didn't care; he's just a little more deliberate. Also, he knew I spent most of my waking hours with Jordan and recognized some abnormal behaviors. Tony understood that my motherly instincts were driving my need to find answers.

Over the course of our marriage, we've come to realize that our differences lead to a balance that is good, not bad. Tony will reassure me that "Everything's going to be okay," while I will push him a bit, saying, "We've got to act."

Times like those reminded us that God had brought us together, not despite our differences, but because of them. We both love the Lord and want to serve Him. Our Christian beliefs are our common bond. Having said that, we realize that we are very different.

That became evident on the nights when Tony was sound asleep while I was still poring over manuals and medical books, looking things up and then calling my mother to get her thoughts. As a nurse practitioner, she had a lot of wisdom and experience in the medical field. I wanted to pursue any leads right then—not wait until the next day. I'm not the kind to sit back and wait to see what the doctor says. That was especially true when I saw daily changes in Jordan's health. He would be strangely fatigued and prone to mood swings or sudden changes in temperature. Tony was far more content to wait on the doctors.

Specialists at the University of Florida had pointed us toward a neurological issue, but recommended that we see the specialists at Johns Hopkins, and sure enough, when we went to Johns Hopkins, we finally got a diagnosis from Dr. Thomas Crawford, a pediatric neurologist. Jordan, he told us, had congenital insensitivity to pain with anhidrosis. Jordan couldn't feel pain and he didn't perspire, so he would never be able to regulate his own body temperature.

This was devastating to hear, especially when Dr. Crawford told us there was no cure and that many children with this disease died before eight years of age. As I sat in his office while he explained the diagnosis, I was very emotional and did not take the news well. But Dr. Crawford was optimistic. He told us there were some things we could do to help Jordan beat the odds.

It's funny—we had been focused on the birth mom's health and making sure she took care of her unborn child. Yet in the end we discovered that Jordan's special needs stemmed from a genetic issue that God had ordained.

I kept going back to my belief that God is in control and that His ways are higher than our ways. There were definitely times, though, that Tony and I wondered whether we would be able to help Jordan and meet all his medical challenges. Often, that's when we remembered how the Besteys had showered unconditional love on their daughter, Catherine, remaining joyful because they knew God was in control of their situation. Likewise, we knew that God was aware of our struggles and that He had watched Jordan as he developed in his mother's womb. God knew all that our son would face, so we could have peace about what was ahead for him.

As we moved forward, Tony and I felt we knew why God

had brought Jordan to us. Because of Tony's job and our insurance through the NFL, we were in a great position to help this little boy we loved so much grow and thrive.

I had one other concern for Jordan: our other kids were so much older than he was. Tiara was fifteen, Jamie was thirteen, and Eric was eight when Jordan was born. I felt our youngest son would need a sibling, and so I asked the adoption agency, "Could you keep our files current, letting us know whatever we have to do to keep them up to date so that, when we start this process again, we won't have to start from scratch?"

As I told our attorney, I didn't want Jordan to be an only child. I was already thinking ahead.

Chapter 10
AN UNSETTLED SEASON

'////////////////.

TONY

I never did get the only child thing. Jordan had three siblings.

But I have learned over the course of our marriage that, when Lauren gets a vision, she can be very persuasive. And when she really wants to do something, she will figure out how to get over the rough spots and make it work for us. When we married, I knew how much Lauren loved kids. I also knew that her mom and dad were still adopting children in their late sixties, so I fully expected to have another adoption discussion in the near future.

In any event, about a year after Jordan's birth, the agency called Lauren and told her about a mother who was going to deliver a baby in the next couple of weeks. Since they didn't have anyone in place to adopt this baby, they thought of us. Of course, Lauren wanted to pursue this unexpected opportunity. From there, things moved very quickly because we had already had a home study and background check done for Jordan's adoption. Unlike Jordan's, however, this one happened during football season. While I had my concerns and would have preferred to adopt during the off-season, Lauren was very convincing. Before we knew it, we were preparing for number five. Once again, the process went very smoothly; in fact, it actually seemed easier. Maybe I was learning.

So in September 2001, we welcomed our second daughter, whom we named Jade. Just a couple of days after bringing her home, something happened that would change us, and change our country, forever.

That Tuesday, the eleventh, the other coaches and I were in the film room watching video and preparing for Sunday's game against the Philadelphia Eagles when someone stuck his head in the room and said, "Man, a plane ran into a building in New York—that is weird." And when we were told the second one had hit, I thought, *This isn't weird—we may be under attack. What is going on?* Before turning on a TV or doing anything else, I called home to see how Lauren was doing with Jordan and Jade.

Lauren told me what she had heard. Like me, she had immediately thought of our family. After we had talked, she contacted the kids' schools. Eventually, she joined a long line of other parents who had arrived early to pick up their children from school. We didn't really know what was going on, but she wanted to be with our kids.

The next couple of days were strange. Everyone was tense, not knowing if this had been an isolated incident or if there would be another attack. MacDill Air Force Base in Tampa had been one of the strategic military hubs during Desert Storm. Would it be a target for terrorists? Were we safe in Tampa? All these thoughts were going through our minds in the days after 9/11.

The commissioner postponed that week's games, so as it turned out, we wouldn't play the Eagles until early January—and because we had a bye week scheduled the following week, we wouldn't play another game until the end of September. In the midst of all the uncertainty, we had to rely on the Lord and understand that He is the one who has to protect us and take care of us. It was a good lesson, one Lauren and I would have to remember later that year.

In the meantime, our family was enjoying Jade. She really was a jewel, the perfect baby. She had no health issues and easily fell into a routine. When we put her to bed, she'd go right to sleep and sleep through the night.

Watching Lauren interact with our two youngest was so much fun for me. Because she was a twin herself, Lauren had always wanted to have twins. Jordan and Jade almost became her set. She bought a double stroller and dressed them alike.

People often told us how blessed these children were to be in our family, but we didn't look at it that way. We felt we were the fortunate ones. God was allowing us to use our gifts and resources in a way that glorified Him. Lauren said it was as if God was allowing us to be a part of His Kingdom building.

One thing was certain: we were on our way to having a kingdom right in our own home! There were definitely days when I longed for some peace and quiet in the house. Or when I wanted just the two of us to be able to go do something. But then I would stop and realize how selfish that was.

Adopting Jordan first helped put everything in perspective. We were reassured when we read Psalm 139: "You watched me . . . as I was woven together in the dark of the womb. You saw me before I was born. Every day of my life was recorded in your book" (verses 15-16). We knew that God had created Jordan and Jade. He knew before they were born that they would be our children. Like Lauren, I believe God put them with us because He knew we would be able to take care of them. It was the perfect place for them to be, all part of His perfect plan.

Having two more children helped me in another way. It allowed me to work on my patience. When people watched me coach out on the field, they thought I was always calm and under control, but that wasn't true.

I used to let my temper get the best of me a lot more often. In fact, I was ejected from some of my high school games, but with the Lord's help and my dad's correction, I learned to control my anger publicly. But that person with biting words . . . I sometimes find him lurking too close to the surface.

I fight that tendency to allow my tongue to have its way, and I have to constantly pray about that. It's something I need to keep a check on. It's easy to say, "Oh, you're crazy. That's the dumbest thing I've ever heard." Hurtful words can be painful, no matter who they come from. But when they come from your spouse, the person you love so much, they hurt even more. I've had to learn to fight the impulse to respond that way. Sometimes, I'm sorry to say, harsh words do come out. And when they do, I have to go to Lauren or the kids and say, "I shouldn't have said that. I was wrong. And I'm sorry." It's a battle, and it's one I don't always win.

Yet what I say is so important because once words come

out, I can't take them back. Lauren may know I said something harsh in the heat of the moment or that I was sharing an honest opinion, but if something wasn't said in the right way or at the right time, it is hurtful. Really hurtful. So I've worked hard to get better with that over the past thirty years.

Lauren and I try to be conscious of what we say, not only out of love for each other, but also out of love for our children. They're learning how to relate to other people by watching us and seeing how we settle disagreements. They're also picking up on what appropriate language sounds like. If Mom and Dad say something or use a certain tone of voice, then it must be okay. We want to set the right example for our children.

Lauren

I felt uneasy throughout the fall of 2001, and it was less about the words that were spoken than those that weren't—though the message was coming through loud and clear. Part of the excitement I'd felt in coming to Tampa was due to the Glazers' interest in getting my input into everything. Over the first five seasons, we frequently met for lunch or discussions. They had always welcomed my thoughts and feedback. But now that had shifted, and I felt it.

In fairness to them, I think Bryan and Joel Glazer were feeling a little more confident about how to run a football club, so they weren't asking for as much input from us. When I'd ask one of them about my part in an upcoming event, he'd say, "No, we've got that" or "We'll take care of that." I was told, "So and so is going to handle the new family this time." They took back the credit card I had always used to take new wives to lunch and put someone else in charge of the women's organization.

Also, they told me they could no longer open up the stadium early for our Bible study. I was most saddened by that, since the wives had really been blessed by it. As they tightened up on things, I no longer felt like I was part of the inner circle. Our relationship had cooled and was more businesslike. It was an uncomfortable feeling.

On road trips, I noticed the Glazers hovering together in the front of the plane. They no longer included us in their conversations as we traveled, and I began to feel uneasy. When I watched them with Tony, I could see that their body language with him seemed different—less open, more distant.

Something definitely was going on—maybe they were starting to go in a different direction and we weren't going to be included in the new plans. I felt that same stiffness with some of the people on staff; they, too, were just a little more businesslike with me than usual. Because I thought we had always had a very good, open relationship, I asked some of them, "Hey, what's going on? Are you feeling what I'm feeling?" And their response was always, "Oh no, no, everything's fine. Everything's great. No, don't worry, we're happy." They tried to reassure me but I just didn't feel it.

All season long, I heard rumors of different coaches being considered to replace Tony. In the midst of all these subtle changes, Tony continued to work as hard as ever. I felt such sadness and betrayal. In fact, it was a real low point in my life because I could see the handwriting on the wall. And I felt so bad for my husband.

I talked with Tony about it. I said I no longer had the peace I'd once had. I no longer felt confident that everything was going well. I even asked him, "Are you sure they're happy with your performance and your coaching?" I just felt like we didn't have the owners' full support.

Tony didn't see the changes in the same way. Early in the season, he'd been aware of talk in the media that, if the Bucs didn't get to the Super Bowl that year, the Glazers were going to make a change. He asked Joel Glazer at the beginning of the season if the rumors that the Glazers were interested in Bill Parcells were true. Joel assured Tony they weren't. "You are our coach, and we have confidence in you," Joel said. Tony took him at his word and didn't give it much thought after that. He told me he was sure the Bucs would have a great year and everything would work out. He was focused on getting the team ready. Not only that, he believed God had a plan for us when we came to Tampa and was confident that His plan was for us to succeed in a big way. With that mind-set, he didn't worry much about what other people were thinking or saying.

That shouldn't have surprised me too much. I knew Tony tended to be a little more optimistic about how things will work out, while I tend to be more realistic. I am also better at reading people's body language. For instance, when Tony and I meet people on the street, I can usually tell which ones are simply zealous, excited fans and which are starting conversations because they have ulterior motives and want something. Tony isn't always able to see that.

TONY

Over the years I have learned to listen to Lauren. She's been right a lot, and now I trust her instincts much more than I did early in our marriage. As it turned out, she was right about the Glazers. They were preparing to make a change.

As the season wound down, however, I had to deal with an even bigger blow. The Thursday before our final regular season game, Rich McKay walked out to the field during practice with a message from my dad. My mom had died at their home in Jackson, Michigan. She was the first of any of our parents to die.

We sat the kids down in the living room to tell them. Everyone took it hard—especially Eric, who cried uncontrollably. When he walked over to Lauren and sat in her lap, it hit us that this was the first time our kids had lost someone close to us. We'd always felt blessed that both sets of parents were still happily married and that our kids were able to know the love of all four grandparents.

My mom had been battling diabetes for several years, so we'd seen this day approaching. We just didn't recognize how quickly it would come. When my parents had come down for a game in 2000, my mom had fallen in a restaurant and broken her hip. From then on, she spent most of her time in a wheelchair.

During that off-season, Lauren had told me, "Your mom isn't able to get around on her own anymore. If anything happens to your dad, we need to have her come and stay here." That was a special moment—I felt such joy that Lauren felt that way.

After learning of my mom's death and talking with Lauren, I decided to coach that Sunday. I knew my mother would have wanted me in Tampa for the last regular season game. That was the first time I really didn't care whether my team won or lost. My mind was on my mom's funeral and the upcoming opening playoff game. Philadelphia beat us that Sunday, 17–13, but the game had no impact on the standings.

Our family flew to Michigan the following day for the funeral on Tuesday. As sad as it was for me, the funeral was a great celebration of my mother's life. Many of her neighbors and former students talked about the impact she had made on them. It was very touching for me and for our entire family.

Less than a week later, we would face the Eagles yet again in the first playoff game. The Friday morning that we flew to Philadelphia, the *St. Petersburg Times* ran a leaked story, which included inside information stating that if we didn't win the game on Saturday, I would be fired. I planned to ask Joel Glazer about it, but he wasn't on the plane. In fact, none of the owners were.

That's when I knew Lauren was right. The Glazers had flown with us to every road game since I had been there, and yet no one in the family was traveling with us to a playoff matchup? All the speculation over the last few months was probably true. Lauren asked a staff member, "What's going on? This is really awkward." But the guy replied, "No, everything's fine. No, you're good, you're good." But when she came back to our seats, she told me she felt as if he'd been brushing her off too.

I was disappointed, but I still felt the Lord was in control. So I wasn't worried about what would happen if we lost. Where would I be the following year? Where would our family be? That was up to Him. But I was disappointed that the owners had said all along everything was fine and then, once I learned the truth from a newspaper article, didn't even want to face me.

After all we'd been through together, the Glazers didn't tell me what they really thought. If they knew I had to win three playoff games or get to the Super Bowl to keep my job, I would have liked them to simply tell me that on day one. That would have been fine. But to tell me everything was good when it wasn't . . . that was very disappointing.

We ended up losing that game on Sunday. I flew back to Tampa, waiting to see if the newspapers had been right. Two nights later I had a five-minute meeting with Bryan and Joel Glazer, who told me they were firing me. It was a pretty quick and cold ending to a six-year relationship, but there wasn't much more they wanted to say. By the time I had driven home to tell Lauren the news, I was ready to move forward.

Had my mom not passed away when she did, I might have spent more time thinking about being fired and how it happened. But when she died and I saw how emotional my kids were, losing a playoff game and losing my job didn't seem to be as big a deal. I think everything happened in the order it did to remind me what was truly important in life.

Now, being different emotionally from Lauren is great in that she and I have been able to complement each other. But in this case it led to some tension. My thinking was, *Well, we have to forget about the Glazers, move forward, and find out what's coming next. There's no point in worrying about what happened.* On the other hand, Lauren was deeply hurt. As she told me, "We've put in six years, and after all we've tried to do, it's not as easy as saying, 'Let's move on.'"

Lauren

I did feel despondent and let down. I had felt like we were part of the Bucs family—a family from which the Glazers were divorcing us, if you will. Tony was already looking ahead, but I was grieving and I was upset. I felt that, by not being upfront with us, the Glazers had shown a lack of integrity. For so many years, we had worked together, resolving all the problems and challenges along the way. Then, all of the sudden we were excluded and, yes, it really hurt.

We tried to model positive behavior for the sake of our children. We prayed about it and told them that it was all in the Lord's hands. They saw us trusting the Lord. Even so, Jamie, in particular, was quite upset. He had such a strong attachment to so many of the players and coaches that he really felt the sting. Tiara was the least upset, since she had carved out an identity separate from the Bucs anyway. Eric was young and couldn't voice his feelings as well.

Still, in spite of our disappointment, even I was able to keep perspective on things. All I had to do was consider what we'd been through in the past four months. Just after we brought Jade home, we'd gone through 9/11, a tough season, and the death of Tony's mom—all before Tony was fired.

What would be next? During our first five years in Tampa, everything seemed to go right. Now we couldn't lose our faith in God because we were going through a tough year. We just needed to focus on where the Lord would take us next. Would we stay here in Tampa or move again to take another job?

We had to focus on the Lord and try to determine what He wanted us to do. We had come to love Tampa by this time, and we weren't sure we wanted to move. We didn't have to take another coaching job; maybe God was trying to get us to see an opportunity in Tampa outside of football. We were trying to figure it out.

Tony invited the coaches to our house shortly after he'd been fired. He talked with them about what was going on and what might be in store for them as a group. He told them he didn't have any answers. He wasn't even sure if he was going to continue to coach. Then he read Psalm 37, which talks about how God protects and cares for His children in times of trouble. One verse, in particular, seemed to strike a chord with everyone: "Be still in the presence of the LORD, and wait patiently for him to act" (verse 7). The others agreed that this verse was a great reminder that the Lord was going to take care of each one of them.

Tony ended the night by telling his staff that he had gotten a couple of feelers from teams and would keep them posted as to what was going on. He said that if he took another coaching job, he wanted everyone to come with him. In the meantime, he said he understood if they looked at other jobs since he couldn't promise them anything. We were going to let God direct us, he told them.

And, though we didn't see it yet, He already was.

Chapter 11

LONG-DISTANCE MARRIAGE

TONY

As personally disappointing as it was to be let go by the Bucs, life had to go on. When our family ran out of milk, I still had to run out to the store to pick up a gallon. And when the Bucs took back the company car I'd been driving, I had to replace it.

Like any busy dad, I try to combine errands when I can. One day on the way to the store to pick up milk for Lauren, I decided to stop by the local car dealer as well. Lauren had talked about wanting an Escalade, but my uncles had worked in Detroit on the car plant assembly lines, and I knew from them that the Escalade has the same body type as the Tahoe. I also knew that a Tahoe was a lot cheaper than an Escalade.

After shaking hands with the salesman in the Chevy dealership, I said, "I want to skip the preliminaries. Just give me your best price on a Tahoe." I knew I was saving about thirty thousand dollars by going with that model over the Escalade, and a lot of our players had purchased vehicles from this dealership. When I asked him to give me his best price, I trusted he would. The salesman went to talk with his manager, came back out, and gave me what he said was his best offer. I paid it, picked up the milk, and drove home. I couldn't wait to get there and tell Lauren about my great decision. I felt like I had gotten her a big enough vehicle to handle all our needs while also saving us a ton of money.

I think her first response at seeing me was relief. After all, she thought I'd just run out for milk, but I'd been gone way too long. I think she liked the way our new Tahoe looked too. But I noticed any signs of enthusiasm drain from her face when I told her that I'd accepted the first price the salesman gave me.

"What?" she said. "Nobody does that! You never pay the first number the salesman throws out. They always start by saying they're giving you their best price. But they know everything's open to negotiation. I bet you could have saved at least a thousand dollars! Why didn't you call me or Loren? We would have told you," she asked. Lauren's dad was in real estate. Growing up, she and Loren had heard all about property negotiations around the dinner table.

In fact, her twin brother called me as soon as Lauren told him about the Tahoe. "It has a sunroof, right?" he asked. "Anthony, tell me it has a sunroof."

"No," I said. "It doesn't have a sunroof."

"It has to have a sunroof. Nobody in Florida drives around without one," he said. "You'd better go back and get one with a sunroof."

I didn't. And to this day Lauren thinks I paid too much for the basic model without a sunroof, but we still have what I refer to as our "gallon of milk car." It's been cross-country; in fact, it's been driven all the way out to Oregon. Lauren may think we lost money because I didn't negotiate, but I feel like we gained thirty thousand dollars because I didn't get an Escalade.

Lauren

Twenty-nine. At most, Tony saved twenty-nine thousand. And the dealer would have thrown in a sunroof if only Tony had asked. But the Tahoe story goes to show what happens when a couple coming from different backgrounds and different perspectives navigate life. We just see things differently.

Fortunately, Tony and I have learned to pray and listen to each other when we have to make major decisions. And one was just around the corner. About the time Tony replaced his Bucs company car with the Tahoe, we had begun talking together about whether Tony's days in football were over. We both loved Tampa, and we weren't sure God was directing us to leave this city we'd come to love. We were happy with our church, the schools, and the community. We thought perhaps Tony should work full time with Family First or Abe Brown Ministries. In my heart, though, I didn't feel that Tony was ready to close the chapter on football just yet. After all, he was just forty-six.

We knew that only a couple of head coaching openings were available in January 2002, and a few of those had already been filled. Tony told me the only viable possibilities he saw for us were Carolina and Indianapolis. Deep down, I'd been hoping Tony might get the head-coaching position in Carolina. I knew a little bit about the Panthers, and I was familiar with Charlotte, where several of our friends lived.

One day when we came home from running an errand, I noticed the light flashing on our answering machine. I stopped for a minute as I began playing it, but since it was for Tony, I called him in. I left the room as he sat down to listen. I came back in to discover that the message went on and on.

"Who was that?" I asked when it finally ended.

Tony told me that it was Jim Irsay, the owner of the Indianapolis Colts, and that I needed to listen to all of it.

"I really want to talk to you, Tony," Jim said. Though he rambled a bit, Jim poured out his heart as he talked about himself and the organization. He ended with a plea: he said he wasn't calling Tony to arrange an interview. He knew he wanted Tony to be his head coach.

Jim's message was refreshing and very encouraging. It felt so good to hear from a team that appreciated Tony's talents and really wanted him. His message left me feeling bittersweet because I was still sad and disappointed about the way things had ended in Tampa with the Bucs. So though I felt a little unsettled, I was anxious for Tony to at least check out the Colts. While I wasn't thrilled about the idea of moving to Indiana, I'd come to love Tampa so much that I'm not sure I would've been all that enthusiastic about any city—even Charlotte.

Tony did fly to Charlotte to interview with the Panthers, but as he continued talking with Jim Irsay, it became clear that he resonated with Jim's vision for the team as well as the Colts' presence in the community.

I told Tony to take his time making this decision. We needed to pray about this opportunity for a couple of days. While Indy seemed like a good choice, there were so many unknowns, which made me nervous. We had to rely on our faith and God's promises to lead and guide us. I was thrilled that Tony had a job offer, but I wasn't sure this was what the Lord wanted. For several days we sought the Lord's guidance and wisdom, asking Him, "Where do you want us?"

TONY

Something had changed for me that last year in Tampa. Though I still enjoyed coaching and appreciated the platform the NFL gave us, for the first time I wondered whether God was trying to let me know He had something outside of football that He wanted me to do.

When I called Jim Irsay back, I discovered that he was even more engaging and captivating live than on tape. He told me that I was his number one choice to coach the Colts and that I shouldn't worry about money or anything else. He just asked me to visit so I could see for myself what a good fit Indy would be.

Jim Irsay pretty much convinced me of that on the phone. I loved what he wanted to do with the franchise. He said that winning was definitely his goal but that he wanted to do it the right way, with the right kind of people. The Colts had been in Indianapolis for less than twenty years, and he wanted to increase the team's presence in the community as well.

I talked with a few people about the Colts' situation, and they confirmed what I was thinking. A good friend of mine, Clyde Powers, worked in their personnel department, and he told me that Jim Irsay was the real deal. Once I met with Bill Polian, the Colts' general manager, I was sold. Bill explained how they had built the offense around Peyton Manning. While they planned on adding pieces to the defense, most of the salary cap money would continue to be spent on the offense, supplying the weaponry to complement Peyton. They thought that, with my background, I could help the team make the most of the Colts' defense.

I told Lauren my feelings, and we agreed that going to work for the Colts was the right decision. I couldn't help but think back ten years when Lauren had felt left out of the decision-making process just before we moved to Minnesota. This time I made sure we had more time for dialogue and prayer. And even though she might have preferred Carolina, she felt good about going to Indianapolis.

There was still one more family decision for us to make, though. I would have to head up to Indianapolis immediately to begin work. That in itself was nothing new; coaching jobs always change hands in January, so whenever I'd taken a new position in the past, Lauren had waited until the end of school year to bring the kids to our new home. This time, however, we had another factor to consider. Tiara was a high school junior, and she wanted to stay in Tampa and graduate with her classmates.

I could empathize with her. When my dad took a job teaching physiology at Delta College, which was about 125 miles away from Jackson, I was going into my junior year in high school. At the time, my older sister, Sherrie, protested that she couldn't miss graduating from high school with all her friends. I had played sports with my buddies since sixth grade and didn't want to leave them either. So my parents decided we would stay in Jackson and my dad would commute for a year. Sherrie was ecstatic, and I was happy about it as well. Of course, the next year I brought up the same argument my sister had raised. So one year turned into two—and then three more years as my parents decided my younger brother and sister should finish school in Jackson too. My dad ended up sacrificing to let all of us finish at our high school. Here I was, a generation later, facing the same situation. I said, "If my dad could do it while holding the family together, and if it's important to Tiara to finish here, we can do it. We can sacrifice for a year or two."

Lauren and I agreed it wouldn't be an ideal situation, but technology would make it much easier to stay connected. We would be making a lot of phone calls and racking up frequent-flier miles, but it was the right decision for our family. One bonus for me was that my sister, Lauren, her husband, Wesley, and their two girls had recently moved from Kalamazoo, Michigan, to Indianapolis. They had actually wanted to move to Florida to be closer to us, and I remember being so disappointed when things hadn't worked out for them to come to Florida. Instead, Lauren took a position overseeing the high-risk pregnancy department at an Indianapolis hospital. It was a real blessing for me, especially that first year, to have Lauren and her family in Indianapolis.

Meanwhile, my wife had her hands full in Tampa. She had to parent five kids largely by herself, trying to meet all their social, emotional, spiritual, and academic needs. But it was almost as tough on me because after work I had to go home to an empty house. I'd call and talk to Lauren and the kids and do my best to be a dad from long distance. I didn't go out a lot because it wasn't much fun doing things alone. I found that if I wasn't careful, I stayed at the office working much later than I needed to.

Taking on too much was not a new challenge for Lauren and me. Over the years, as our family grew and the number of activities grew along with the number of kids, Lauren and I realized we had to be aware when we were running ourselves down. We had noticed that a lot of our disagreements—especially the major ones—occurred when we were tired. Whether at the end of a long road trip or a week too packed with events, we'd be more prone to snap at each other because we were simply exhausted. Eventually we learned to stop such arguments and say, "You know what? Let's revisit this in the morning when we are a little fresher and a little less tired."

We both know the biblical mandate not to go to bed angry. Ephesians 4:26 says, "Don't sin by letting anger control you. Don't let the sun go down while you are still angry." While some people view that as a hard-and-fast rule to resolve conflict immediately, we came to realize that there are times when just agreeing to disagree until the morning is the wiser course. It's not that we want a disagreement to linger or fester, but sometimes discretion seems to be the better part of valor. We definitely had to practice this at times during the months I lived alone in Indy.

I know the older kids recognized that I was sacrificing for them, but Jordan and Jade were so young they only knew they missed their dad. I wanted them to realize I would rather be there with them and tried to tell them that as often as possible. We all looked forward to the summer when I could return to Tampa for a number of weeks and we could be back together as a family. In fact, Lauren and I decided not to accept any speaking engagements in the summer of 2002, and we've continued that practice to this day.

We would never have considered this living arrangement if we felt our marriage wasn't strong enough to withstand it. Putting that much distance between a husband and wife normally isn't good, so Lauren and I don't recommend it for all couples—especially those early in their marriage. But we had been married twenty years and felt we were strong enough, unified enough, and committed enough to make it work. In addition, we both felt it was the best decision for our children.

Because of my work with the NFL, Lauren and I had been forced at times into a long-distance relationship. We got our first taste of it when she and I began dating and I was at the Steelers' training camp all week. I remember racing down the highway after Saturday's camp so I could be with her that same evening. In those days, I often had no desire to eat or sleep because I was falling in love with Lauren and couldn't wait to be with her.

Those intense feelings of infatuation didn't last, of course— just as they don't persist in any couple's marriage. And it's probably good they don't. Nobody could function day after day, month after month, year after year if his or her thoughts were consumed with another person all the time. As Lauren and I discovered, marital love matures and deepens over the years. To endure, it's got to be built on a solid commitment to the other person and the life you've built with each other rather than on your feelings, which may go up and down.

I compare it to playing in a football game. You start off with energy fueled by adrenaline for the opening kickoff. You're so pumped up, and there's nothing like it. The whistle blows and you find yourself flying down the field 100 miles per hour. But you don't have enough adrenaline in your body to keep the emotion at that level for sixty minutes. You have to calm down a little bit and play the rest of the game.

So many problems in marriage occur when spouses notice that the intense physical attraction is no longer there and assume that must mean the love is gone. They figure either they've changed or the other person has changed, but in any event, they're no longer getting the instant emotional payoff they had at first.

Lauren and I lived apart for about eighteen months when I was in Indy, and it was tough. One of the biggest challenges for Lauren was trying to keep me connected to the kids while keeping them on a regular schedule. At the time, Indiana didn't observe daylight saving time, so by the time I was free in the evening, the kids were often heading to bed in Tampa. She had to be creative to make it work. I think our love brought us through. But that's not to say those months were fun. Often our love had to be sacrificial, with Christ as our center and the source of the stamina and patience we needed to make family life work. We kept praying together as a couple, even if it was only briefly on the phone. That helped us to stay unified, even when we were living miles apart.

Lauren

By the time we decided that the kids and I would stay in Tampa, Tony and I were committed to each other and to making our living situation work. We'd learned long before that without commitment, we were setting ourselves up for disappointment. Life isn't always going to be easy and we wouldn't be sustained by loving, wonderful "feelings" every day.

During the 2002 season, I flew to Indy every weekend,

which was a challenge. The kids came some of the time, but Jamie was playing football, so he couldn't always go. Eric was in elementary school and hadn't started playing yet. He loved the Colts games and always wanted to come with me. On Friday night, we'd cheer Jamie on at his football games and then fly to Indianapolis the following morning.

When the team was playing at home, Eric and I would head to Tony's apartment to get a little rest before the game. When the Colts were playing away, as soon as we'd arrive in Indy, we'd hop on the team plane and fly to the opponent's city. We'd fly back to Indianapolis with the team after the game and then catch the late flight back to Tampa. Many times Eric and I would have to run through the airport to get on that last flight to Tampa at 9:05 p.m. Whew! It was exhausting, but I always wanted to be there for Tony. I was usually worn out on Monday mornings when it was time to resume my role as mom and dad in Tampa.

The off-seasons were easier for me because that's when Tony was able to come to us in Tampa. He tried to give his staff one week off per month, which enabled him to get home to us too. He also flew home on weekends. That was how our give-and-take worked. During the season, I had the grueling schedule, and in the off-season, Tony did all the traveling.

We also spoke on the phone every night. I tried to arrange a time each day when Tony could talk with the kids, too, but that was more challenging. He and I could always talk late at night, but we had to find time between the kids' activities and Tony's work schedule for them to talk during the day. Too bad we didn't have access to texting like we have now.

While the hectic schedule wasn't a surprise, keeping the

family in Tampa while Tony worked in Indianapolis provided me with some challenges I hadn't anticipated. The Bucs, led by their new head coach Jon Gruden, won the Super Bowl the year after Tony left. It was tough not being part of that.

As they advanced to a 12–4 season and toward the playoffs, many Bucs fans felt free to tell me, "No offense, but . . ." Then they would say how the coaching staff was really getting the team on track. "Your husband was just too nice and couldn't get the job done."

I tried to shelter the kids from such comments. I had the support of our church and my friends, but the public can be very fickle and free with their comments. It was difficult to listen politely, even though for the most part I knew they felt no ill will toward Tony.

Jamie once told me that kids would say to him, "We're glad that the Bucs got rid of your dad. We have a winner now." He was very sensitive and would often come home in tears after hearing their strong remarks. It hurt him deeply to hear people talk about his father that way, so I worked hard to encourage him. In fact, I think trying to keep the kids happy, grounded, and with the right attitude helped me get through those times too.

Sometimes the kids received support from unexpected places. For example, one of the teachers at Berkeley, Eric's school, was Kathy Gruden, Jon's mother. One day Mrs. Gruden took Eric aside and told him that the Lord clearly needed his dad in Indianapolis to do His work, even though it had been disappointing for our family. Tony and I appreciated the kindness she showed to our son and were grateful that she had reached out to him.

As I focused on the well-being of my family, I appreciated the support I received from loyal friends. Most of all, I drew strength and encouragement from God's Word. For instance, I clung to the practical advice and promise found in Philippians 4:6-7: "Don't worry about anything; instead, pray about everything. Tell God what you need, and thank him for all he has done. Then you will experience God's peace, which exceeds anything we can understand. His peace will guard your hearts and minds as you live in Christ Jesus."

As we headed into the 2003 season—our second year apart—I reminded myself that Tony and I had made the decision we felt was best for our family and that our heavenly Father would help us weather this storm.

Chapter 12

TOGETHER AGAIN

///////////////////

TONY

October 6, 2003, was special for two reasons: not only was I with my family for my forty-eighth birthday, but the Colts were playing the defending Super Bowl champions, the Tampa Bay Bucs, on *Monday Night Football*—in Tampa! No one could have written a script like that.

Lauren dropped the boys off at the hotel where the Colts were staying so they could go to the stadium on the team bus with me. She and Tiara would drive to the game later.

It was my first trip back to Raymond James Stadium, and the night was much more emotional than I'd expected. My mind flooded with memories as I walked around the field during pregame warm-ups, shaking hands, exchanging greetings, and chatting with former players and assistants. I wasn't sure what to expect when my name was announced during team introductions—the opposing coach is usually either booed or ignored—so the crowd's welcoming ovation meant a great deal to me.

The warm feelings didn't last long though, as the Bucs came on strong. At halftime we were down 21–0. Though we came out and scored on our opening drive in the third quarter, the Bucs quickly drove for another touchdown. We narrowed the spread when we scored a touchdown just after the start of the fourth quarter. But the game seemed headed to a disappointing finish when Ronde Barber picked off a pass from Peyton Manning and ran it back for another Tampa Bay touchdown with just over five minutes left in the game. We were now down 35–14. I hoped Lauren had left by that point because the Bucs fans had already started to celebrate. I knew how hard it would be for her to watch that.

Just before our offense was set to go back on the field for the kickoff, I considered taking Manning and the other starters out of the game to make sure they didn't get hurt. Tom Moore, our offensive coordinator, suggested we let the starters make one more drive. Four plays later, we scored, making it 35–21. Unbelievably, we would score two more touchdowns in a little over three minutes, tying the game and forcing it into overtime. Well after midnight, we kicked a field goal to win, 38–35. It was the biggest fourth-quarter comeback in *Monday Night Football* history.

Lauren

That was an emotional night for all of us. It was the first time I'd been back to the stadium since I'd cleaned out my suite the year before. Before the game, Tiara and I met a group of our friends in the parking lot to tailgate. As I rushed up to greet them, I was surprised to find that most of them were wearing Bucs gear. Perhaps noticing the hurt in our eyes, they sheepishly said that they were lifelong Bucs fans, and while they loved the Dungys, this was *Monday Night Football*! They would cheer for us next week, but not that night.

I had thought our friends would be cheering for us and the Colts, especially since some of them had asked us to get them tickets to this sold-out game. Fair or not, it felt to me as if some of our best friends had moved on from us after the Bucs won the Super Bowl with Jon Gruden.

I was grateful for the warm welcome Tony got from the fans, but the one I received was much colder—literally. In fact, as Tiara and I made our way to club seating, people were throwing Cokes at me. Security told me they couldn't help, saying, "Sorry, but these fans have been drinking all day and are out of control." The real reason, I suspect, was the Colts gear I had on. Then, as the Colts took a beating during the first half, some fans suggested I leave and go back to the cornfields in Indiana. By this time, I was more concerned with protecting Tiara than with watching the game.

I felt sick when the Colts fell behind by three touchdowns. By the fourth quarter, most of our friends had left, not wanting to rub in the lopsided score. Even most of the hecklers were leaving us alone by this point. Still, there was no way I would leave early. One of the rules in our family was that we would meet Tony right after the game, no matter what. I wanted to consistently show my support for him, win or lose. And we did get slaughtered some games. But Tony knew that after he met with the team and did his interviews, we'd be outside the locker room waiting for him.

Tony has always been good about putting any loss behind him, and I was still planning to have our normal family reunion after the game—even though the mood might not be the greatest. Of course, our emotions soared after the fairy-tale ending of that game!

As Tiara and I left the stands, a number of people seated near us asked me if I could help them meet Peyton and Tony—after they'd given us such grief during the game. And the security guys, who couldn't be bothered and had refused to intervene earlier, suddenly were on top of things. They even wanted to follow me to the team buses after they escorted me down to the locker room. (I guess they'd finally decided to do their job.) All of a sudden I had a big extended family, and everyone wanted to celebrate with us.

But this was going to be a time just for our family and our team. Tiara and I had a surprise birthday party to set up. We raced to the waiting area of the stadium to roll out the huge sheet cake decorated in the Colts' colors of royal blue and white. This was going to be a night to remember!

TONY

Once the candles were lit on the cake, all the players, coaches, and staff celebrated the win and my birthday. I've always known Lauren was my biggest fan, and she shows it over and over, in ways both big and small.

We finished that regular season with a 12–4 record and we made the playoffs for the second year in a row. We advanced to the AFC Championship game before losing to the New

England Patriots. It was a bittersweet ending to a strong year. The team was getting more involved in the community, and we were making strides on the field. Best of all for me personally, the family moved up to Indy after the school year ended and Tiara had graduated from high school.

Lauren and I had some discussions about our living situation in Indianapolis. We knew we'd eventually return to Tampa, so we didn't want to sell our house there. At the same time, I wasn't sure how much longer I'd be coaching the Colts. My goal was to lead the team to a Super Bowl victory; then I might be ready to retire. The Colts seemed very close to winning one, so we decided to rent a home in Indianapolis.

That fall, Tiara started at Spelman College in Atlanta. Jamie was a high school senior, Eric was in fifth grade, and Jordan and Jade were in preschool. It was so good having the family back together. Times were fun. As soon as the little kids jumped into our car after school, they started talking a mile a minute. By now, Eric had quieted down, and he couldn't understand why they were so noisy. He said that it sounded like we had Alvin and the Chipmunks in the car, and he often put on headphones to drown out the chatter of his younger siblings. He wouldn't believe it when we told him he was once exactly the same way.

In the midst of the good times, God gave us a couple of reminders of how fragile and precious life is and how quickly things can change. Just after the draft that spring, I'd been startled by a phone call from my dad telling me that during a routine physical, his doctor had been alerted to an abnormality in his blood tests. After further testing, he was diagnosed with leukemia.

My sister, Lauren, recommended a fantastic cancer hospital

in Indianapolis, and my dad was admitted immediately. Over the next two months, I was able to visit him almost every day. Sometimes we talked about life and the kids; at other times, we just reminisced. It was a special time. My dad responded well to treatment, and the cancer went into remission. Unfortunately, just before he was due to go home, he developed an infection. Because of all the treatments he'd had, his body wasn't able to fight off the infection, which spread very quickly. In less than forty-eight hours, we went from anticipating his release from the hospital to watching him pass away.

It was quite a shock and certainly something I hadn't expected. My dad had been doing so well, and we had been praying so much. But it was the Lord's time to take him. He'd lived a long, full life, and I'd enjoyed many fun times with him. He had given me a lot of great advice over the years, and it was hard knowing that I wouldn't be able to talk things over with him any longer.

Lauren

The second incident happened as Labor Day was approaching, which meant that not only had the kids gone back to school but football season was right around the corner. I was enjoying the end of summer and trying to build a sense of camaraderie among the Colts' wives, just as I'd done with the Bucs' wives. One way we were doing that was by working out together at our local health club. Not only did our daily spinning class keep us in shape, it allowed us to bond as we enjoyed one another's company and talked about our families.

One evening while Tony and I were taking our evening walk, I suddenly started to have difficulty breathing. We had been strolling casually—not even power walking—but I couldn't get enough air. I felt like I was going to suffocate. Even Tony, who is usually so calm, became alarmed and contacted the team doctor. X-rays revealed that I had a collapsed lung and needed surgery the next day. The doctor said that collapsed lungs tend to hit two groups of women: those who smoke and those who are athletic. It never crossed my mind that my workout routine of running and swimming could put my health at risk. It was startling to go from the picture of health one day to flat on my back the next.

Since the Colts had just started their season and Tony was busy, my family jumped into action. My mom packed her bags and had Loren drive her to Indy so she could help with the kids and manage the household. Jamie and Eric were helpful, too, as they realized they had to pitch in a little more since I was going to be sidelined for a while. They helped my mom navigate around town and do the grocery shopping, and they helped bring Jordan and Jade to the hospital to visit me. I missed my family dearly and looked forward to their visits. The two operations required to repair the collapsed lung were successful, but I needed extended physical therapy afterward. It took a while, but as the fall progressed, I began to feel better and gradually got back to my normal routine. We all tend to take our health for granted, but this was a timely reminder that good health is a blessing from the Lord and we need to be thankful for it!

Because of the death of Tony's dad and my sudden illness, Tony and I became even more committed to talking to our children about the importance of family relationships and the need to cherish every moment with one another. We knew the Bible says that tomorrow is not promised us, and these crises caused that truth to hit home for all of us.

TONY

One downside to my job as a football coach was that I couldn't always be as available as I wanted during difficult times. I was very thankful for my mother-in-law's help, as well as the support from our Colts family and our church friends. They were all there for us, helping our family and supporting us every step of the way until Lauren was feeling better.

When you're in professional sports, people tend to see only your on-field life. They think you are immune to the normal trials that everyone goes through, but that is far from the truth. Our entire family had to cope with losing my dad and dealing with Lauren's major health scare. But those trials pulled us closer together and gave us a chance to talk to Jordan and Jade about God and His sovereignty. After all, we had prayed for Grandad and he did not get better, but we also prayed for Mom and God did heal her. We emphasized that even when we can't explain why God answers our prayers the way He does, we can't lose faith in Him. He does hear us, even when our requests aren't answered the way we would like.

During the 2004 season, the Colts were learning and growing as well. Once again, we finished our regular season with a 12–4 record. Then we lost in the playoffs to the Patriots for the second consecutive year. Maybe Lauren was starting to have doubts about that Super Bowl. Maybe, just as when we were first married, she simply wanted to live in a house that fit us. But whatever the reason, I was excited when she started to get comfortable with the idea of living in Indianapolis and talked about buying a home.

As a measure of how close we had grown, Lauren let me put an offer on a house without her even seeing it. We had started looking at homes, and one day when she was out of town, our realtor was taking me around. He showed me one particular house that I really liked, and I described it to Lauren over the phone. She said we should go for it and put in an offer. I hesitated, thinking, *I really like it, but what if she doesn't? She really needs to see this first.* The realtor also said he thought Lauren should look at it before making an offer. He told me he thought the house was too dark—kind of like a man's house.

But by then I knew Lauren's taste. We'd spent time looking at model homes and open houses just for fun and as a way to see what features builders were putting into homes. I told Lauren about the home's large, fenced-in yard and described the lower level, which seemed like an ideal place for the kids to play. I also described its location on a cul-de-sac in an attractive neighborhood. After hearing my description and looking at a few pictures of the house online, Lauren told me she trusted me, and if I liked it that much, we shouldn't take a chance on someone else beating us to it. She felt we should make an offer. Before she'd even seen the house, our bid was accepted.

Lauren

When I did get to look at our new house, I saw right away that it was perfect! I was so proud of Tony for selecting our lovely two-story home. After so many years of marriage, I think couples really do understand each other's preferences and can confidently rely on each other to make those kinds of decisions. Now, ten years earlier I wouldn't have had that much confidence in Tony picking out a house. At that point, I'm not sure if he would have understood the dynamics of our family and what we needed.

That spring, we moved into our new home and were finally together again (except for Tiara, who was studying sociology at Spelman College). We needed to purchase new furniture because we had left most of ours in our Tampa house. I started decorating right away because I wanted to make the house a home quickly. Not only was our home a place where the children could welcome their friends, but I envisioned Bible studies, informal get-togethers, and fellowship taking place there. I picked up many decorating tips from visiting model homes and open houses with Tony. This was a hobby we have grown to enjoy over the years.

Working on the house, getting the kids acclimated at their schools, and keeping up with Colts functions and activities kept me busy well into the fall. I didn't even have time to notice that it was September and already nippy outside. The kids were wearing coats and jackets while their friends in Tampa were still wearing shorts and summer clothing. Sandals had long since been replaced with boots and closed-toe shoes.

Tony and I enjoyed getting back into the routine of taking walks together regularly. We also found a great bike trail close to our new house. Perhaps we were trying to make up for those eighteen months that we were apart; in any event, we were always looking for activities we could do together to stay fit and active.

In fact, we have always tried to find common interests. Growing up, I'd been athletic but never followed professional teams closely. That had changed. Not only was professional football Tony's job, but he always seemed to be watching something sports related at home. Over the years, I've tried to watch with him. And throughout our marriage, he's looked for things he could embrace that I enjoy. When we lived in Minnesota, that included camping. He also began visiting model homes in local "parade of homes" events with me so we could discuss ways to make our house more inviting and attractive.

That's not to say everything clicks. For instance, I love to read and discuss books, but Tony doesn't. The idea of a book club pains him, though I've belonged to many during our marriage. Whenever I come home from book club, all excited about the discussion and characters in a novel, Tony is likely to look up and say, "That story didn't really happen, so I don't know why you think this is fun. You just spent four hours talking about some fictional people who don't exist and didn't really do what you read. I don't get it." But I love it, even if Tony doesn't. I've encouraged him to try it but haven't made much progress over the years. It's just an area where we're different.

Of course, you won't find me spending six hours on a fishing boat rocking around in the Gulf either. Tony's dad had introduced him to fishing as a boy. When we moved to Florida, where he could fish in the Gulf of Mexico and numerous freshwater lakes, Tony's love for it reached new levels. That was great for him. As for me, no thanks.

Still, we were so grateful to be together again that it felt natural to search for areas of common interest. Our plan was simply to be together and take things one year at a time. Tony still enjoyed coaching, and he loved working for the Colts. However, his twenty-fifth year of coaching was approaching, and he'd told me he knew he wouldn't be doing it forever.

Coaching was all we'd ever known as a couple, but as much as we loved it, it wasn't everything. And when a couple is involved with such a demanding career, they do make sacrifices. Our years with the NFL had been tremendous, a great season of our lives, but I knew Tony was not going to be like some men who coach into their sixties or seventies. At some point, he would retire and move on to the next season of his life.

I didn't think that winning a Super Bowl would define Tony's success as a coach either. He'd worked so hard and I wanted him to win a championship, but we needed to think about how long was enough. I believed our family was missing out on some things because Tony had so many demands on his time. That was something that I had been in prayer about for quite some time, but, ultimately, I knew the decision was his.

At about this time, Tony told me he was beginning to wonder what God's plan was for the future of our family. We both knew He had one, and we wanted to follow it. We just had to keep listening to His voice.

Chapter 13
REMEMBERING JAMIE

////////////////////////

TONY

On the field, everything was clicking for the 2005 season. We had a really good team and we knew it. In the back of my mind, I felt there was a good chance this would be my last year of coaching. It wasn't that I was close to being burned out; it had just been on our minds since we were fired in Tampa—when would be the right time to start doing other things?

I believed with all my heart that God meant for us to be in Indianapolis and for me to coach the Colts. Just not forever. Football is such a tough schedule. Even though I'd been in charge of the itinerary and planning over the last ten years, I still had to work every day from July to February, including Thanksgiving and Christmas. That's just how it is.

I knew Lauren wanted to have me home more, and I was

certainly looking to her for wisdom. Together we were going to figure out the right time for me to retire from coaching. And we had a feeling that time might be approaching.

In fact, Lauren and I thought we might have God's plan all figured out. My fiftieth birthday, my twenty-fifth year in coaching, and our first Super Bowl could all be part of the Colts' 2005 season. We thought early 2006 might turn out to be the perfect time to step away from the NFL and move back to our home in Florida. Jamie, who was interested in studying criminal justice, had already returned to Tampa that fall to enroll at Hillsborough Community College.

Yet Indianapolis was home to the rest of our family right then, and we were still committed to building friendships there. As always, our top priority was finding a church where we could worship and fellowship with people who didn't care about our association with the Colts but simply cared about us as individuals. We were looking for a church that had both solid Bible teaching and an established children's program, so all our kids could grow spiritually.

Many people recommended an Indianapolis megachurch that drew people from all over our metropolitan area. Though we visited and agreed that the pastor was a fabulous communicator, we were looking for a smaller church. We found one in a church that had actually been planted by that larger church. New Life Christian Center had started with three hundred original members, and we felt right at home there. We became good friends with the pastor, John Ramsey, and his family. But Pastor Ramsey was so dynamic that the church quickly grew to a couple of thousand members. As exciting as it was to see God at work there, we wanted to belong to a smaller church body.

Eventually, we discovered Northside New Era, which was similar to the churches we'd belonged to in Pittsburgh and Kansas City. With a membership of about four hundred people, it felt much more intimate. We appreciated the warmth of the pastor, Clarence Moore, as well as his solid teaching. We were able to make friends with many families with young children, and nobody treated us differently than anybody else. Once again, we felt like we were part of an extended family.

Looking back, I realize that searching for the right church has been similar to finding the best doctors for Jordan. Lauren has a very good sense of what fits us and the environment in which the kids will thrive and grow best. Whenever I allow her to take the lead in these decisions, our family usually finds the right spot.

As our family was settling into our new home in Indianapolis, the Colts were having a stellar year. I reached a personal milestone in October when I won my one hundredth game as a coach. By mid-December, our record was 13–0, and eight of our players had just been named to the AFC's Pro Bowl team.

I'm grateful we were plugged into a church and together again in Indianapolis, because while all was well on the field, heartbreak was looming right around the corner.

Lauren

Three days before Christmas 2005, the phone rang in the middle of the night. I handed the phone to Tony because most of our late-night calls were work related. But this time, it wasn't. The police in Tampa were calling with some devastating news about our second-oldest child, our son Jamie. For reasons we'll never understand, he had taken his own life.

That late-night call was totally unexpected. This was our precious, tender-hearted Jamie, the most compassionate and loving of our children. The Jamie who was always befriending those without a friend—kids of all shapes, sizes, and backgrounds; not just tall, athletic, confident types like him. This was the child who brought home lost animals of every variety. This was the boy, so like my dad, who never met a stranger.

From our first moments of disbelief and sorrow to the outpouring of love and support we received at Jamie's funeral four days later, Tony and I clung to each other in the fog of those first days. The pain and sorrow were indescribable, but because of our faith in God, we were able to hold on to our foundation—communication and prayer—through a very dark time.

Our Christian beliefs never wavered, but knowing that Jamie's place in heaven was secure didn't make it any easier on us. We knew we weren't promised a life without trials, and we had to cling to God's promise that He was with us. We had to continue to hold on tightly to the Lord's presence in our lives and our commitment to each other.

As time passed, we realized how important it was for the two of us to be available to support each other. Maintaining communication was so important. We'd seen others walk through trials like this, but frankly, nothing prepares you for it. We had to find our own way through. We learned, for instance, that we needed to talk about what had happened, but we each needed to do that at different times of the day. For me, it was often in the middle of the night when the house was quiet and the kids were in bed. It was then that I most needed to talk with Tony. He always made sure he was available to hear my heart, even as we talked about the same things over and over. We discussed all the difficult questions of how we would go on from here and the questions that had no answers, such as what went wrong and what we could have done differently. Those issues inevitably came up, but we couldn't dwell on them since there were no answers.

Tony knew our talks were essential to my healing and my way of grieving. I am much more emotional, and for that reason, it seemed harder for me to work through my pain. Tony and Jamie were close, but our mother-son bond was so strong. We were two peas in a pod, and he was truly a mama's boy.

Our family received a lot of support—cards, notes, phone calls—but I wasn't comfortable responding to them. I wasn't comforted by talking to others about our loss; I wanted to grieve privately. The only people I wanted to talk with about Jamie's death were Tony, our pastors and their wives, my mother, and Tiara and Eric.

I learned that when you're looking to help someone, you have to be sensitive to the timing. On some days, I would be really down and sad, and Tony or others helped carry me along. Other times, I would be doing okay and suddenly our loss would hit Tony. As those people closest to me reached out, I found it helpful when they mentioned a specific time when they would make themselves available to talk with me. If I wasn't ready, they understood. But it was better, I found, than a "call me if you need me." I didn't usually follow up on those general invitations.

However, Tony and I had to give each other the space— and the grace—to grieve differently. Though it usually didn't help me to talk with others about our loss, it did help Tony. Also, I knew going back to work would help my husband, so I encouraged him to get back to the Colts and his routine.

Pastors and friends who'd experienced similar losses told us how important it would be to keep the lines of communication open with our other children. That meant staying in touch with Tiara from a distance. Eric was in middle school and wasn't as communicative. Like Tony, he tends to hold things inside. So we worked hard to keep in touch with him too. Jordan and Jade were a little too young to really understand what happened, and we could tell them only that Jamie had died and was now in heaven. All in all, the fact that our kids were of all different ages and were recovering in different ways forced us to talk more as a family.

We were aware that people all over the country were watching how we responded to Jamie's death. We wanted them to see how our faith was sustaining us and how God was helping us get through this storm. We could feel the prayers for us. We still do. What held us together in the end was the knowledge that we will see Jamie again and we will be reunited. We have something to look forward to, and that always draws us back to a place of peace. No matter how much pain we were feeling, whenever we got those sinking feelings, we could always come back to our faith in Christ.

That's not to say we've ever fully recovered from Jamie's death. You don't ever get over the death of a child; you learn how to get through it. You move forward, taking steps of healing—sometimes small steps—each day. Driving past the Pizza Hut where Jamie worked was really hard the first few times. But rather than viewing the overwhelming emotions as a setback, it was helpful to recognize them as progress, knowing that future trips past places that triggered memories of Jamie would bring less intense and more reflective, often joyful memories.

When a child is in your life for nearly nineteen years, you don't get over it. You do a lot of praying and reading the Bible, but it's something that you never, ever get over. If you haven't experienced the death of a child, the grief is hard to comprehend. Jamie's death changed our lives so that we would never be quite the same again.

TONY

Even when Lauren and I became testy with each other, we knew it was critical that we listened to each other. It was tempting to get frustrated with her when she was having a good day and I wasn't. *How can you act like nothing happened?* I'd find myself thinking. Then, a day or two later, our roles would be reversed. It would be a while before our family got back to "normal," but in the meantime Lauren and I tried our best to move forward and not look behind us.

I had always been quick to talk publicly about my Christian beliefs and to praise God for all the good things in my life. Now I knew Lauren and I would have to stand up and say that, while everything wasn't great and everything wasn't perfect, we still trusted the Lord. We still believed He had our family's best interests at heart and that He was there, not just in the pleasant times but in the tough times as well. God had given us some tremendous blessings, but He had also been with us through firings, congenital birth defects, and the death of my parents. We had to remember that as we pushed through.

At the end of the day, the feelings of grief didn't just magically go away. They needed to be felt and experienced, and over time, they did become less intense. Our situation also reminded us of the importance of living in the present. We knew from the Bible that we weren't promised tomorrow, but Jamie's death illustrated that very clearly for us.

Denny Green, who was coaching the Arizona Cardinals at the time, had come in from Phoenix for Jamie's funeral. He gave his condolences to Lauren and me and told us how much he would miss Jamie.

"Thank you. Thank you for that, and for no regrets," I said.

Denny looked puzzled.

"I'm realizing that so many parents go through loss and grief," I told him, "but looking back, I don't have regrets over time missed with Jamie. He was young when I was your assistant, and you fostered such a family environment. So many times Jamie could be with me at practice and training camp. That gave me so much time with him, so many times that I told him that I loved him. . . ." My voice trailed off.

Denny hugged me, and as I hugged him back, I was so thankful that he had been my boss during Jamie's formative years.

At Lauren's encouragement, I returned to coaching two days after the funeral. I wasn't sure that was best, but she didn't see what good staying at home would do. We just needed time.

That Sunday, we played our last regular game of the season. With that victory, we finished the season 14–2. Unfortunately, we lost our first playoff game to the Steelers, even though we were playing at home and were heavy favorites. For our fans, it was an incredibly disappointing end to the year. Yet as a family, it was much like the 2001 season after my mom died and we lost to the Eagles. Because of Jamie's death, we were more than able to keep the defeat in perspective. It was, after all, just a football game.

So the plan we had been so sure of earlier in the season didn't materialize. There was no fairy-tale ending to the season, as you might see in the movies. We were able to take some time together after that loss to Pittsburgh, and for our family, that was probably more important than continuing to win playoff games.

We also entered 2006 knowing that God had walked us through many smaller difficulties and problems during our marriage. We had prayed through those, and we realized that God had heard us and gotten us through each and every trial. We just had to put our faith into practice again—and understand that God's plans aren't always the same as ours. I had thought this would be the year to retire, but that perfect ending I had envisioned never materialized. Lauren and I agreed we couldn't stop at that point. If we did, people would think I was retiring because we'd lost our son.

Lauren

We knew Jamie wouldn't want Tony's coaching career to end that way. We didn't think God would either. And while no one could ever replace my sweet, fun-loving Jamie, as we headed into 2006, God knew I had room in my heart for a child who needed a mother's love.

In 2005, I had a chance meeting with Joel Kirsh, an Indianapolis adoption attorney, at Eric's school. We chatted about Jordan and Jade and talked about my passion for children. In the spring of 2006, Joel called to tell me about a birth mother who wanted to place her child for adoption. He asked if we'd be interested.

We definitely were open to learning more. For several months, Tony and I had talked about adopting another child. We had discussed it with the kids, and everyone was ready.

When Joel said he might have a baby for us, we all felt God's timing was perfect.

Actually, Tony would say the timing was completely perfect except for the timing of our son's birth. I had taken our younger kids to my mom's for the weekend right before Justin was born. When Joel called, Tony agreed to meet him to pick the baby up, but he assumed he and Eric would simply settle Justin in at home until I got back. Instead, when he called me, I said, "Please bring the baby to Pittsburgh so my family can see him. They want to meet and welcome our new addition!"

Tony was petrified at my request. "How can I get into the car with a newborn baby and drive six hours with just Eric to help me?" he asked.

I told him, "You manage fifty-three rough, tough football players every day, and you can't make it six hours with a baby who will eat and sleep and not give you an ounce of trouble?" I was laughing so hard that I think I embarrassed him into bringing the baby to Pittsburgh.

As soon as Tony and Eric drove up to my parents' house, I scooped up baby Justin and excitedly introduced him to Grandma, Pop Pop, and all the relatives. I could tell Tony was just happy to be there and proud of getting the boys there on his own.

Later, he confessed to me how afraid he'd been that Justin would cry all the way and he'd be unable to do anything about it. He knew he couldn't count on Eric for any help—he was even more fearful of babies than Tony was! Tony fed Justin just before they left, and the baby slept all the way to Pittsburgh. While Tony breathed a sigh of relief when he arrived in Pittsburgh, I was just grateful I hadn't received a phone call from him telling me he'd turned around halfway into the trip!

Chapter 14

CHAMPIONS

////////////////.

Lauren

The 2006 season was a fun one—at least by the end. Yet I knew the drive to training camp in Terre Haute that summer would be a tough one for Tony. For the first time in years, he went alone, with no boys in the car. Eric was entering ninth grade, so he now had high school football practice. And Jamie had gone with Tony to every camp in Minnesota, Tampa Bay, and then Indy. Tony had always looked forward to taking the boys to training camp with him. This year he would be alone.

Life was a little more hectic for me at home. Not only did I have a new baby in the house, but I now had to juggle Eric's busy sports schedule while making sure Jordan and Jade stayed on top of their schoolwork as well as their soccer, swimming, basketball, and other extracurricular activities. It kept me on the go, but I loved it.

At least once a week, I would pack a nutritious dinner, pile the kids in the car, pick Eric up at school, and head to the park. We'd eat dinner together before dropping Eric off at his evening Bible study group. It was important for the kids to share their day with each other and fellowship with one another. We may have spilled a lot of food and stained the seats with drinks, but we enjoyed a lot of laughs in the back of the family car. When the weather got colder, we continued the same routine—except that we ate together in the car, motor running, along a quiet street. In addition to taking the kids places, I was meeting new friends through the kids' school activities and trying to get involved by volunteering at the kids' schools and at church, teaching their Wednesday night classes.

Our family enjoyed watching Eric's high school football games. Most Friday nights during the fall, we proudly donned our red, black, and white and headed to the football field. We waved the "Dungy" banners that the younger kids had made and cheered wildly for number 15 as we sipped thermoses of piping hot chocolate.

And the Colts were winning, too, which extended the excitement during those weekends. Sundays after church, now dressed in blue-and-white attire, we headed off to the RCA Dome to cheer for Tony and our beloved Colts. No wonder I was always worn out by Monday morning!

Indianapolis was having another winning season, but it was different from 2005 when the wins seemed to come so easily. This year the team was just scraping by, finding new ways to win. Every game was a struggle, whereas in 2005 the Colts dominated nearly every team. On the other hand, the games were more exciting because they were closer. I didn't mind that, as long as we kept winning.

Unfortunately, after winning their first nine games, the Colts lost two of three before heading to Jacksonville in early December. They lost that game, 44–17. Tony had never taken losses too hard, but this one affected him even less than it would have before.

However, it was the worst Colts defeat in almost five years, and a lot of fans were panicking. Many said that Tony needed to get upset, to show some emotion. A few even suggested that he "give the players a piece of his mind"—you know, do something to shake things up. But he didn't. He always maintained a calm, professional attitude.

TONY

I had learned from Coach Noll that a setback like this one was a good time to simplify things, not a time to make a lot of changes. We just needed to relax and stay the course.

Not only that, but I'd been reminded again early in the season to work hard but keep things in perspective. During a game late that September, Reggie Wayne caught a touchdown pass in the final minutes against Jacksonville to win the game for us. When we got to the locker room there was a message waiting that said Reggie's brother had just been killed in a car accident. On the heels of Jamie's death, it reminded me that there were plenty of things more important than winning football games. It also made me remember that we should never take relationships and family for granted.

Throughout our December slump, I felt that football would get back on track. And it did. After winning our last regular season game against Miami, we found out we would be playing the Kansas City Chiefs in the first round of the playoffs the following Sunday. The Chiefs were coached by our longtime friend Herm Edwards.

During that week, Lovie Smith, coach of the Chicago Bears, called to ask me for a couple of tickets to the game. He wanted to attend with his wife, MaryAnne. I knew Herm would bring his wife, Lia, so Lauren and I talked over the idea that we all meet for dinner the night before the game.

We had all worked together in Tampa, and even though we were separated by many miles, we remained close. Herm, Lovie, and I were all head coaches now, and each one of us was blessed to have a team in the playoffs. Lovie's Bears had a bye that week, so he and MaryAnne were able to drive to Indy to watch our game. It was a great reunion. We reminisced, laughed a lot, cried a bit, and ate too much.

Over dinner we talked about old times and how far we had all come from those days at One Buc. We passed around family pictures and expressed amazement at how much our kids had grown. Those little kids, who once filled up on Gatorade and chased each other around the practice fields, were now college students.

I listened as Lauren and Lia laughed about how they had unsuccessfully tried to play matchmaker with our daughter and the Edwardses' son. The guys didn't discuss much football, but we hoped that two of us would meet in the Super Bowl. As we left the restaurant, Lauren told me she'd been thinking about how good and gracious God had been to all of us.

The next day, we beat Herm and the Chiefs, which was bittersweet. The following Saturday, we went to Baltimore and beat the Ravens to put ourselves in the AFC Championship game again. We would play the winner of the San Diego Chargers–New England Patriots game, which would be played in San Diego the next day.

That Sunday I faced a work versus family dilemma. Our kids had asked us to take them to Chuck E. Cheese's after church on Sunday, and we had agreed. But I didn't want to miss the football games being played that day. The Bears were playing their playoff game at 1:00, and I wanted to watch and root for Lovie's team. The Chargers-Patriots game would be on right after that at 4:30, and I really wanted to watch that game to find out who we would play. It was especially important because if San Diego won, we would have to go out there to play them, but if New England won, the game would be in Indy.

We got home from church and watched the Bears beat the Seattle Seahawks in overtime. It was such a thrill to see Lovie get his first playoff win. But through it all, the kids were clamoring, "When are we going to Chuck E. Cheese's?" Knowing that we had promised this outing to our kids, I had to do what was right. As tempted as I was to say, "Why don't you guys just go without me," we all jumped into the car and headed to Chuck E. Cheese's.

Fortunately, the restaurant had the game on when we got there. I noticed a number of other dads keeping one eye on the game while also enjoying the craziness and their kids. Everyone in the place let out a yell when the Patriots hung on to win. Since that night, I've always had a special place in my heart for Chuck E. Cheese's.

Lauren

The AFC Championship game was now scheduled to be played in Indianapolis, and the fans were just wild all week. By the time we arrived for the game on Sunday, the mood in the RCA Dome was electric—and very loud—for the game against our nemesis. Unfortunately, it got quiet quickly. New England jumped out to an early lead: 21–3 in the second quarter. I couldn't believe it. We were playing at home, and we had so much momentum. It wasn't supposed to be like this.

Our team kicked a field goal right before the half to cut it to 21–6, which gave Colts fans some hope. We played a wonderful second half, but with two minutes remaining, we were still trailing by three points. Then Peyton Manning led us on a clutch drive, and with a minute left, we scored a touchdown to win the game, 38–34. We were going to the Super Bowl!

The Dome went crazy. Fans jumped up and down with excitement. The field quickly became a sea of blue and white confetti. All of us Dungys and Harrises were crying tears of joy. I thought of all those times I'd sat in the stands, feeling helpless because I wanted to help Tony and the team. What a wonderful feeling it was to watch them, knowing we were all going to the Super Bowl. That same day we learned the Bears had defeated the Saints and we'd be playing Lovie and the Bears.

But that night, we weren't yet thinking about the Bears. We were ready to celebrate. It took Tony much longer than usual to get out of the locker room, but we would have waited for him all night! We passed the time congratulating players and staff and talking about how much fun it would be going to Miami for the Super Bowl. A family member had taken our younger children home, but it was well after midnight when our group of twenty-five family members and friends walked over to Palomino's Restaurant to celebrate. They had agreed to stay open for us, but nobody expected we'd arrive that late.

It was snowing outside, but that was one time the cold didn't bother me.

The staff at Palomino's was great. They went out of their way for us as we talked, ate dinner, and replayed the game. I didn't want the night to end, but finally at about 3:30 in the morning, Tony had to break it up. He and the team had a Super Bowl game to prepare for.

TONY

We spent a magical week in Miami. I had played in Super Bowl XIII with the Steelers twenty-eight years earlier, but I couldn't believe how much bigger the game had grown. (I'd attended the game the year after we played but then vowed never to go again until I was playing in it.) So much was going on, and so many fans came in for the festivities.

The team went down the Monday before the game. Lauren came with the kids on Thursday, and we had a wonderful time. By the time my family arrived, most of the team's preparation was done, so we were able to spend time together. On Friday night, we took the kids to the NFL Experience, which featured football-related games and entertainment and was open to all Super Bowl ticket holders. We overheard people marveling that the Colts' head coach was there two days before the big game. But for us, it was like any other Friday. It may have been the Super Bowl, but that didn't change the fact that it was a football game, and Denny Green had taught me that we needed only three days to get ready.

Many family members and friends had come to Miami to cheer on the Colts. Both Lauren and I missed our dads. I knew how much my dad would have loved to be there. Lauren's dad was having health problems and had to watch the game from home. But the rest of the Harrises came in full force!

Lauren's twin brother, Loren, was there, as he had been for so many games. He didn't like to fly, so he would often jump in the car after a hard week of work and meet up with our team. It didn't matter where the game was being played—somehow he always managed to be there. And that weekend, like every other game weekend, he wanted everybody to know that he was my brother-in-law.

Lauren and I found time to stay grounded and pray in the midst of the craziness of the weekend. With our downtime on Friday and Saturday afternoons, we continued with business as usual in our relationship. We didn't put things on hold just because it was the Super Bowl. One of the things we discussed was what to say if we won. We knew that I had a tremendous platform all week long, and if the Colts were victorious, that platform would become even bigger. We wanted to give honor and glory to God in the aftermath, and we were excited about the possibility we might be able to use that platform to speak to millions of people.

Sure enough, after another rocky start, we came back to win the game 29–17. Lauren had to sit through the rain the entire game, but she didn't care. And for the first time ever, she didn't wait to meet me outside the locker room. At the final whistle, she left her seat and went down to the railing. Once she caught Jim Irsay's eye, he escorted her right down onto the field. The next thing I knew, she was standing up with me at the podium, pumping her fists in front of thousands of fans.

I did get to thank God on the victory podium. CBS announcer Jim Nantz asked me about being the first African

American coach to win the Super Bowl, and while I told him I was proud to represent so many coaches of color who had gone before me, tonight was for Indianapolis. I also said that after all that we'd been through, we were very pleased to have won while doing things in what we believed was the Lord's way—embracing family and the things that truly mattered. That was special. And then we were escorted back to the hotel to the team party and continued the celebration. As you can guess, no one wanted to leave.

We finally got back up to our room around 3 a.m. We had to pack everything up and get ready for the flight home. The kids dozed off one by one with smiles on their faces and blue paint in their hair, but Lauren and I never went to sleep. We stayed up reminiscing, just the two of us talking about the incredible journey. And missing Jamie . . . and my parents.

Before we knew it, our family had to head to the airport to fly back to Indianapolis. The city had planned a victory parade for Monday afternoon. It was so cold—five below zero—that we figured the crowd wouldn't be huge. But the streets were jam-packed. Then as we were getting into our positions for the parade, we couldn't find Jordan.

We finally found him about fifteen feet up on the canopy of the main float with Peyton Manning and the rest of the big-name stars. I don't know how he got up there, but he wanted to ride on the top with the players. I guess he was taking after his uncle Loren! It was a struggle to get him down and convince him to ride with us.

As we rode through the city and saw how many people were impacted by the Colts' success, I felt so great. I couldn't believe how many people had braved the cold to be out there on the streets, cheering and supporting us. Then we pulled into the stadium and found that it was packed, too, with fifty-five thousand people. My brother-in-law Wesley is our unofficial family photographer, and he was there snapping pictures to help us remember it all.

When the players, staff, and I finally got to the stadium, I had a chance to thank the fans who'd rallied around their team. "You guys are awesome," I told them. "For the last sixteen or eighteen hours, we've been enjoying this championship. We had a team party last night, but we were looking forward to coming home. This is more than we could ever have expected. Thank you for this turnout."

Immediately after the parade, Lauren and I agreed that it seemed like the right time to retire. But a few days later, we no longer felt that way. Just as retiring after Jamie's death might have sent the wrong message, we felt retiring now might do the same thing.

I'd always told the players that winning a Super Bowl wouldn't change their lives—but knowing the Lord would. Lauren and I agreed that if we retired, we'd be reinforcing the wrong message. Not only that, but I felt I was in a better position than ever to make the claim that an NFL team can win a championship even if its players and coaches maintain a healthy balance between their work and family lives. I'd always preached that message, but it obviously carried more weight after our Super Bowl win.

Later that year I also wrote *Quiet Strength*, a book that I'd hoped would have an impact on people, especially sports-minded boys. It turned out to reach even more people than I could have imagined—far beyond simply sports-minded boys—and I found the letters from readers quite moving. The book's success created a new platform that I couldn't have anticipated the Lord opening for me.

I planned to stay one more year after winning the championship, and we started the 2007 season well. We were undefeated and shooting for our eighth win of the year when the unbeaten Patriots came to town. A couple of days before the game, I recorded a public service announcement for The Villages, a children's home in the area. Unfortunately, our unbeaten season came to an end a couple of days later, and I'm sure some people would have said that I shouldn't have taken the time to record any PSAs during the season, or at least not before a game between two unbeaten teams.

We finished the regular season 13–3, but when we lost to the Chargers at home in the playoffs, I wondered if that game would be my last. Then Jim Irsay asked if I would coach the 2008 season to open the new stadium, Lucas Oil Field. He'd been so good to us that I told him I'd think about it, just as a favor to him.

So I coached one more season and retired after the 2008 season ended. Each year Lauren and I analyzed whether it would be our last, and that last fall we agreed that she would take the children back to Florida to prepare for our next phase in life.

Lauren

One of the reasons we brought the family back to Tampa in January was to give the kids time to get acclimated to their new schools. That was a focus of mine every time we moved. And because we recognized that each of our children had distinct strengths and challenges, this often meant enrolling them in different schools, sometimes outside of our zoned district. Finding the right school was especially important for Jordan because his teachers had to be aware of the physical challenges he faced and the special accommodations he required. We applied for a special admission and then had him placed in a wonderful school, Lutz Elementary, where his special needs would be met by a loving support staff. Jade and Justin were enrolled at Carrollwood Day School, which had a strong academic program and was conveniently located five minutes from our house.

The decision about where Eric should enroll presented a slightly different challenge. After four years in a small, private school in Indianapolis, he expressed a strong desire to attend a public school when we returned to Tampa. Jamie had attended Gaither High School, but we didn't feel Eric would be comfortable going to the same high school that Jamie had attended. I was particularly interested in Plant High School because of its academic reputation, and the school district agreed with our request and gave him special admission to Plant.

Although Tony and I were focused on the academics and school environment, Eric was pleased to learn that the Panthers had an excellent football program and he was excited to get started with his new team. Unfortunately, someone in the community wasn't quite as excited and expressed his displeasure.

Soon after Eric had enrolled at Plant, I received a disturbing, hate-filled letter in the mail that caught me and Tony off guard. The letter said Eric shouldn't try out for the football team because too many blacks were coming to Plant and taking spots from the white players. The anonymous writer threatened trouble for the entire family unless Eric left Plant immediately.

Tony and I were very concerned and immediately contacted the police. Our family felt vulnerable and under attack by this disturbed individual. When we shared the situation with Eric, he broke down and cried. As a mother, it broke my heart to see my child so upset and confused by the hatred directed at him.

A few days later, we received a second hateful letter, but this one included stronger racial overtones. It was discomforting and alarming to think that someone could be so upset by Eric's enrollment that he would target our family. While we didn't want our lives to be dictated by some anonymous, hate-filled individual, we were extremely concerned for Eric's safety. The threats of harm and violence were real. We were not going to back down and leave the school, but we knew we needed to take precautions and reported the second letter to the Tampa Police Department. At that point we contacted NFL security, and they offered to escort Eric as he traveled to and from school.

Though I believe God is in control, I remained nervous and on edge, even after we'd taken all these precautions. My faith was definitely being tested. Our pastor and committed praying friends lifted up this situation in prayer daily along with us. But in quiet moments, I found myself asking, Are we doing the right thing by allowing Eric to continue at Plant? Will God honor our prayers and provide a blanket of protection for our child? Will He prevent any harm from coming Eric's way? My stomach was in knots each morning when Eric kissed me good-bye. Even though he was escorted by security to school, I worried until he returned home each evening.

The threatening letters continued for a couple of weeks, with each one strongly warning me to do the right thing and remove my son from Plant. Then, one day, we received a call from the Tampa police. They had arrested the man who had sent the letters. We were told that he had also sent anonymous letters to several other African American players on the team. I was truly relieved and grateful to God that He had watched over the boys and that none of them had been hurt.

And this situation, as alarming as it was, gave us another opportunity to dialogue with our kids during family meetings. We discussed the fact that everything in life isn't perfect. We will all face situations that are challenging and difficult to comprehend, and there are certain people in this world we will never understand. We prayed for the man who'd sent the letters, asking that his hardened heart would change. But in the end, we had to trust in the Lord and have faith that He would guide and protect our family, no matter what the challenges.

TONY

Jim was extremely generous to us that final year, allowing me the use of his private plane to come down on Fridays to watch Eric play football at Plant and then flying me and my family back up to Indianapolis for the games. It was just like old times—a lot of travel and some tired bodies, but it was worth it.

Though our decision hadn't been set in stone, Lauren and I had felt confident going into the 2008 season that it would be my final year coaching. While it would have been great to end my career with a second Super Bowl victory and relive the excitement of that 2006 season, we didn't get that storybook ending. My last game as coach of the Colts was a playoff loss to the San Diego Chargers in January 2009. It was finally time to retire.

As I left to walk from my office to the press conference to announce my retirement, Jackie Cook, my assistant, handed me a letter to read. A family had wanted to tell me about the child they had adopted.

From The Villages.

As a result of seeing my 2007 PSA, taped before the Patriots game.

It was the last letter I received as a head coach, and one of the most touching notes I have ever gotten. It seemed like a perfect way to close my coaching career, a reminder that the Lord will bless whatever platform we happen to have.

Chapter 15

NEW ARENAS

///////////////////.

TONY

What would come next? It was amazing that, as much as Lauren and I had talked about retirement over the last few years, we didn't have any definitive plans when it came.

My main priority was to be an effective and involved dad and husband. I loved waking up and being able to help get the kids ready for school and to assist with car-pool duties. Watching Eric play football during his senior year was so enjoyable for me that I never experienced any regrets over leaving coaching. I missed my players and being around the coaches, but I never missed the job.

At the same time, I knew I was responsible for managing the platform God had given me. I just wasn't sure what that would look like. Lauren and I received plenty of suggestions from other people, many of whom had something they felt I should do. I may have had no more off-season player evaluations to complete, no more NFL league meetings to attend, and no more scouting trips to take me away from home, but I was suddenly getting calls, e-mails, and letters from all over, inviting me to come to various events.

Once again, I had to determine what to accept and what to turn down, since the offers were coming from so many great causes. For instance, it was exciting to see fifty kids give their lives to Christ after I spoke at a Fellowship of Christian Athletes meeting. That definitely benefited the Kingdom. Yet did that mean I should travel 365 days out of the year to speak to young people? No. Working with my family, spending time with my kids, and being a husband to my wife was still my primary job. I had to think back to what Tom Lamphere had asked me: "What things can only you do?"

During this time, Lauren and I prayed together a lot. We asked God to direct us and help us be in agreement about which opportunities He was calling us to pursue. We asked with confidence since we'd prayed together for five years about when I should retire. Now we both felt God was telling us, "I've got some new things in store for you, and you've got to trust Me for them. Don't worry about other people's opinions. Just try to listen to Me." At that point, we weren't sure where the Lord was leading us, but we had peace about that first step. (Oh, I also noticed a soft voice telling me, "Lauren needs warm weather!" I wasn't sure whether I was hearing from God or Lauren on that point, but we did return to our home in Tampa.)

Another opportunity seemed to present itself near the end of my final season. The day before our last playoff game in

San Diego, I met with the network commentators who would be broadcasting the game. That's nothing new—one of a head coach's responsibilities is to meet with the commentators for a production meeting before the game. They discuss items, such as game plans, offensive and defensive schemes, and player injuries that will help the broadcasters during the telecast.

After this particular production meeting, Dick Ebersol, the head of NBC Sports, stopped me to ask whether I thought that would be my last year of coaching.

I shrugged and smiled.

Then he added, "If you do retire, we'd love to talk to you about broadcasting with NBC."

"Thanks, Dick. We'll cross that bridge when we come to it." I didn't think too much of it at the time—I was focused on the upcoming game.

I had never envisioned myself working in television, but right after the press conference announcing my retirement from coaching, Dick called me to follow up on his offer. He said he'd been serious when he suggested I explore sports broadcasting. "We'd love to talk to you about it," he said.

I wasn't sold on the idea because I didn't think I had the personality for TV and I was worried about taking a job where I'd have to travel. Wouldn't I be getting right back into the situation I had just left?

But Dick was aware of my commitment to my family. He was adamant that as a studio analyst with *Football Night in America*, I would need to be in New York for just eighteen weekends in the fall, never during the week or in the off-season. And he emphasized the platform I would have. He told me that the show's producers would let me do segments highlighting players' outreaches and foundations—even the ministries I was involved in.

It sounded good, but I still wasn't sure. Maybe it was just the fear of the unknown. Or maybe the fear of failure?

So Lauren and I did what we always do when there is a big decision to make—we prayed about it. Lauren encouraged me to explore this opportunity, so I agreed to do the Super Bowl broadcast with NBC as an audition. It was a blast. The preparation and teamwork needed to do a broadcast is so much like getting ready to play in a game. I was hooked!

Broadcasting also reminded me how important good coaching is. In this case, I received a lot of instruction and encouragement from Sam Flood, the show's executive producer. It was similar to what I experienced when I was working for Chuck Noll. Sam is one of the top producers in sports television, but he is very much a family man. While helping me learn the broadcasting business, he has been supportive of our family. Once again, I have been blessed with a boss who shows me that you can be very dedicated, get to the top of your profession, and still keep your family relationships strong and healthy.

After spending a lot of time with me and Rodney Harrison, a former New England Patriot strong safety and the other new cast member, Sam positioned each of us in the way best suited to our strengths. Since Rodney has a strong personality and is very smart and spontaneous, Sam had Rodney react to how a team was playing. My role would be to break down a play to help the viewers better understand why it worked. As we became more comfortable and versatile on the set, our roles gradually expanded.

Before each broadcast, NBC sends me material to review

at home during the week. That is followed by a rehearsal on Saturday evenings. Over time we've gotten to where we can do more and more off the cuff. Just before going back on camera, the producer might tell us: "Tony, you talk about why Seattle's defense is playing well today against Cincinnati, and Rodney, talk about how Cincinnati's offensive players can counter that. We're back in ten. . . ."

Ironically, I think I'm recognized more now than when I was coaching. But I consider analyzing football on TV my job now, and I enjoy it. I especially appreciate the great relationships I have with a new set of coworkers; close working relationships are one of the things I missed most when I left the Colts.

We've also been able to do a number of those segments that Dick had promised. After I attended a fund-raiser for Michael W. Smith's Rocketown outreach center in downtown Nashville, NBC ran a piece highlighting the event and what Michael has accomplished with Rocketown. Two others that stand out to me were segments about Tampa's Wharton High School foot-ball team's "Dare to Be Uncommon" initiative and Pittsburgh Steeler Ryan Clark's efforts to assist his hometown church in Marrero, Louisiana, as it worked to rebuild the surrounding community. Drug dealers had taken over many homes aban-doned by residents after Hurricane Katrina. Rather than fleeing the neighborhood, the church began buying up and rebuilding the properties, as well as constructing a community center.

Lauren

I thought the broadcasting job would be a wonderful fit for Tony. People trust him, and he's great in front of people. I thought he'd do well on TV too. Tony has so much knowledge and wisdom to share from years of playing and coaching. I also didn't think it would be wise for him to give up football cold turkey. The sport had been part of his life for so long. I thought if he got completely away from it, he would be tempted to go back to coaching at some point. Now he'd remain involved in football, maintain the public platform God had given him, and—best of all—spend weekdays and the entire off-season with his family. I couldn't wait to have a normal Thanksgiving and Christmas like everyone else.

And I've enjoyed getting to know Tony's coworkers at NBC too. I go with him to New York on some weekends, and we take the kids there around the holidays. We were also able to attend the Winter Olympics in Vancouver and the Summer Olympics in London as NBC's guests. I especially loved seeing the figure skating firsthand and hearing the personal-interest stories about the athletes and their journeys to make it that far.

Sam Flood has been so accommodating. He lets the boys come to the studio with Tony, so it's almost déjà vu. These days Jordan and Justin are the ones running around the office, getting in everyone's way. They know all the broadcasters and cameramen, just as young Jamie and Eric knew the players and coaches.

Now that Tony finally had some free time, I wanted to enjoy having him at home. But there was one other thing on my mind. Justin was two and a half, and I was feeling the pull in my spirit to adopt again. I don't think Tony was surprised when I mentioned it.

My parents had continued to enjoy parenting into their seventies, even adopting Amanda and Devin very late in life. Tony did point out the math: the fact that if we adopted an infant now, he would be seventy-two years old when his child walked across the stage at high school graduation. But I informed him that age was only a state of mind and we had so much love to give. So later in the summer of 2009, we joyfully made another trip to the agency offices to pick up our sweet baby, Jason Anthony, a precious gift from God.

Tony reminded me that seven represents the biblical number of completion, so he thought Jason might complete our family. I told him I understood the significance of the number seven, but then I brought up Jacob, the patriarch of Israel, who had twelve sons. I pointed out that we weren't even halfway to having twelve boys. I just wanted to let him know I felt the Lord might still wish to bring other children into our family.

As we were adding children, we also branched out into writing children's books. Tony and I coauthored the picture book *You Can Be a Friend*, along with a number of other picture and early reader books for children. *You Can Be a Friend* encourages kids not to judge others based on their outward characteristic but to look at the heart. We feel that is such an important theme, not simply because kids need to learn to include others regardless of such things as appearance, background, or religious beliefs, but also because of what we've learned from Jordan. He has had to learn to be resourceful to find activities to do with friends during the many stints when he's been recovering from injuries or surgeries.

Late in 2011 the Heart of Adoptions agency, the organization in Tampa through which we'd adopted Jordan back in 2000, called us. Jeanne Tate, the attorney who founded the agency, told us about a birth mom considering adoption who felt our family would be a good match for her baby. So in 2012, we brought home our adorable son Jalen. Roughly eighteen months later, we adopted another sweet little boy whom we named Jaden. Tony jokes that if we adopt one more, he's going to return to coaching because it would be quieter and less hectic. But he loves our large family, and the kids are keeping both of us young. We now have seven boys (including Jamie, which we always do) and two girls. The six youngest live at home and keep the household active and lively. Tony and I feel so blessed that God has entrusted these beautiful children to us to nurture, love, and parent. We wouldn't have it any other way and feel privileged that this is the plan He has for us.

Our older daughter, Tiara, just finished an internship with UNICEF and is looking for a permanent job helping young people. In the fall of 2013, Eric began his junior year at the University of Oregon, where he's a gifted wide receiver on the highly ranked Ducks football team. A sociology major, Eric doesn't know what the future holds, but he's a great student and is considering teaching. Jordan, who we were told might not make it to his teen years, just celebrated his thirteenth birthday and is in a mainstream middle school classroom. We are so proud of him because he has overcome so many physical challenges, the latest being his thirty-third surgery, this one to repair a fractured elbow. He often aggravates injuries, to the point of bones breaking, without even realizing it. But he has a tremendous spirit and blesses our entire family with his positive attitude.

Jade is the only girl who is living at home with us and five rambunctious brothers. Like me, she enjoys running, swimming, and biking, and she is the most social of our children. The phone rings off the hook for her with invitations to parties and events. Justin seems to be taking after Eric; like his big brother, he enjoys all sports, especially football. He looks like he has a future as a wide receiver: he loves the game, is a well-rounded athlete, and lives and breathes football. Jason is our sensitive and loving little boy who is just beginning preschool. From the looks of our family room furniture, I think he'll end up playing football or some other contact sport! Our two youngest boys, Jalen and Jaden—my "twins"—are developing a close bond with each other and have their siblings wrapped around their sticky little fingers.

To meet the diverse needs of all our kids, our family joined a large church, Grace Family Church in Tampa, not long ago. Early in our marriage, I don't think we would have been comfortable in a big church and would have had difficulty functioning there. But we've learned to adjust. Tony and I have opened our home to a weekly couples' Bible study with friends from church. We love exploring God's Word. In addition to good Bible-based preaching and small group ministry, we are grateful to have found a church that appeals to teens, grade-schoolers, and preschoolers and that has a great nursery. It is also near our home, which is important since it's gotten more difficult to get all the kids fed, dressed, ready, and to church on time.

TONY

Parenting a number of small children hasn't prevented Lauren and me from finding time to do things as a couple. We started the Dungy Family Foundation with our relatives in Pittsburgh, Indianapolis, and Minneapolis–St. Paul. We're committed to helping individuals and families grow academically, socially, and spiritually. It has been very rewarding, not only to support organizations in Florida, Minnesota, Pennsylvania, and Indiana that share our vision, but also to begin some of our own initiatives, such as our reading program.

After her work with the NFL wives in Tampa and Indianapolis, Lauren wanted to begin something similar again. We approached the school system in Hillsborough County in Tampa, thinking that we'd target the Title I elementary schools (those with at least 85 percent of their students qualifying for free or reduced lunches). Lauren and I have been working our way through these schools by going to two of them each Tuesday during the school year. We read our books to the students, let them ask questions, and talk to them about the importance of reading and writing. Lauren is quick to remind them that even NFL players have to do their homework when preparing for games.

Lauren and I look forward to Tuesdays because it's a time when we can give back to our community in a way that interests us both. And it's also become a "date day" for us. We see our older kids off to school and get a babysitter to watch the youngest ones. Then, after we've read in our two schools, Lauren and I have lunch together. It's just another way for us to make sure we are scheduling some time for the two of us.

I'm also still involved with All Pro Dad, and Lauren is active with iMom, two programs that are part of Family First, the organization founded by Mark Merrill. Lauren and I attend one big event for the group annually and donate a day every other month to shoot videos, blog, or develop other encouraging resources for parents.

Our nightly walks are still an important way for us to stay connected, but now that we have more time, we also enjoy hiking, backpacking, and bike riding. Lauren has become quite the athlete; she's gone from distance running to training for triathlons. She talked me into running a 5K with her, but that's where I think I have to draw the line.

My football schedule once prevented our family from scheduling getaways from late summer through early winter. We always took our annual trip to Black Mountain for the Fellowship of Christian Athletes camp, and we usually went to Pittsburgh for a week to visit Lauren's family. Now we're trying to branch out and see new places and try new activities. At Lauren's prompting, we've been camping and whitewater rafting, and we've visited many new vacation spots. I have to admit I'm often skeptical when Lauren suggests a new "adventure." But the things she plans end up being a lot of fun.

She usually has to talk me into them, though, which she says can be like pulling teeth. But the great thing for her is that we don't have to plan so far ahead. We used to have to think, *The week after the Super Bowl . . .* or *The week before training camp opens. . . .* Now we can say, "Next weekend, let's go . . ."

Over the last couple of years, we've enjoyed spending a lot of time in Oregon where Eric is in school. In fact, that's where we've spent the last few summers. Lauren has even admitted that she enjoys getting some relief from the Florida humidity during our time out there.

In the summer of 2013, we decided to purchase a Winnebago RV so we could explore the West and let the kids experience firsthand what they've read about in history books. We started with a trip south to California where we spent time with Lauren's oldest brother, Kevin, and then we traveled along the Pacific coast. We hiked in the Redwood National Park, taking in some amazing scenery and learning about how the redwoods were able to grow to such a massive size. Our trip reminded us of the driving trips we had taken with our older kids twenty years before—only our vehicle with its slide-out bunk beds was much more comfortable than the minivan we drove in the 1990s.

Lauren met a dad in Oregon who has kept a journal of every RV trip his family has taken. The teacher in her lit up—what a great way for us to learn as we go, while also recording our memories. Initially, buying an RV didn't seem like a good idea since our homeowners association in Tampa doesn't allow residents to keep campers in their driveways. However, once we found a great RV dealer in Eugene, Oregon, that said we could store one on their lot if we bought it from them, Lauren got the ball rolling, and we now have our own RV. We plan on leaving it in Oregon until Eric finishes school. Lauren is looking for a place in Tampa where we can store it once we drive it back there.

Even so, a part of me wondered if it wouldn't have been cheaper to rent an RV for our trips. I guess it's just my nature to look at the practical side. Like with the kids. Every now and then I'll ask Lauren, "Hey, where are we going to be when these kids get off to college? What if we have some health issues later on in life? You know I'll be seventy-five when Jaden graduates from high school, right?"

But Lauren doesn't look at it that way. She tells me, "You've got to trust the Lord. Assume it's all going to be manageable and just look forward." Sometimes I get too focused on the what-ifs, and she points out that if I worry myself to death about things, I might end up doing nothing.

Her philosophy and mine still give great balance to our marriage. We see, more clearly than ever, that some of our different perspectives came from our parents. I can't get mad at that or say Lauren should be more like me. That's one reason God brought us together, and we make good decisions when we work through things as a team. Many times, just as with my NBC job, her perspective helps me look at things differently—for the better.

I see a lot of her mom, Doris, in Lauren. Both are very strong women with a great deal of faith in God. They love kids and enjoy having them at home, even as they get older. They trust the Lord, knowing He will work all things out.

Lauren

Tony tends to be analytical like his dad. He'll say, "We can do this, but here's how we should go about it." He is deliberate and thinks things through before acting. As a result, his plans usually turn out well. We are opposites in a number of ways, but we have learned to navigate our differences. It was harder to do that when we were newlyweds.

When you are committed to sticking it out with your spouse, you find that you learn about him or her—and his or her family—over time. As I interacted with Tony's family over the years, I learned more about him. And the more I understood how they were wired, the easier it became for me to handle some of the differences in our personalities.

Likewise, Tony quickly realized that when he was in the Harris home, he wasn't going to observe many quiet, reflective moments. There would be conversation! That's just how my family is, and that's how they relate to the people they love. As a result, he learned that he was going to have to communicate and talk more when he was with me.

On the flip side, when I began dating Tony, I remember my amazement when I discovered he might not speak to his parents for a couple of weeks. After all, I talk to my mom every day, often several times a day. At first, I asked him what was wrong. "Nothing," he'd say.

And so I learned that nothing *was* wrong with his relationship with his parents. That's just how they were, and it didn't mean they cared about one another any less than my mom and I. That was helpful for me to know once Eric left for college, since he would go several days or a week without calling. I realized that he didn't have to follow my pattern to show that he loved me.

Because of what Tony and I have learned about the effect our family backgrounds had on each of us, we know that the way we relate to each other and the way we handle problems is serving as the blueprint for our own children.

I was powerfully reminded of this last summer while attending the wedding reception of Brad and Sandy, the daughter of one of our family's friends, the Morans. Following a formal ceremony at a historic university chapel in St. Paul, Minnesota, guests headed to the reception hall, where they were invited to kick back while waiting for the bride and groom to arrive. Rather than being directed to our tables, we were encouraged to put on one of a number of costumes that had been provided and then gather in groups for photos. We have a priceless photo of Jade, Justin, and their cousin Alon decked out like rock stars!

The real enjoyment for me, though, came later that evening after the kids had taken off their disguises and the dinner was well underway. As I looked around the room, I had to smile as I watched Jade mingle easily among friends and strangers alike, trying to make everyone feel comfortable and a part of things, much as I've always tried to do. I spotted Justin, who was in the middle of the dance floor with a festive crowd around him. He was moving to the music, working the room while showing off his latest YouTube moves. He reminded me so much of my dad, the life of the party.

Then I glanced at Eric, who looked so handsome in his tuxedo. Seeing him ushering in the wedding of his childhood friend had brought tears to my eyes earlier. Now he was sitting at a table looking subdued, much like Tony's dad often appeared when in a crowd. The evening would wrap up early for Eric since he had to catch a flight back to Oregon. He'd committed long before to participate in an event for the Fellowship of Christian Athletes at the Eugene Emeralds minor league baseball game the next day. It would have been easy to justify finding a replacement for the event, but he felt compelled to honor his commitment. Even though we were sorry to see him leave, Tony and I were proud of him for being a man of his word.

In that moment, I realized how individual every Dungy really is—and yet how powerfully we influence one another. As Tony and I shared some of our marriage ideas and advice with Sandy and her new husband, I couldn't help but think, *My, how time flies.*

None of these ideas about marriage and family came right away. Some of them came only with great pain. But over time, they have helped us find out who we are. And they have helped us get beyond the minutiae and prepare for some of the real challenges to come.

That's not to say we have it all together. Even after thirty-plus years, we're still learning, still growing, and still adjusting.

But we have survived so many stressful events that people say can derail a marriage—firings, moves, losing parents, losing a child, unexpected career changes, and major disappointments. Through it all we've tried to build an uncommon marriage by following two basic principles: staying focused on each other and letting God lead our marriage.

So for better or for worse, we press on, side by side, committed to each other. And we hold on to the belief that if we continue to trust in God, He will lead us through whatever life sends our way.

Afterword

"The heart of marriage is memories."

So says actor and comedian Bill Cosby. We think he is on to something; in fact, that is why we've shared the story of our three decades together. We've opened our hearts to you in the hope that you and your spouse will strive for an uncommon marriage, too, whether you've been married fifty years like Bill and Camille Cosby or are newlyweds, like our family friends Brad and Sandy (Moran) Pulles. As you know from our story, an uncommon marriage isn't a perfect one; it's simply the union of a man and a woman who commit to staying together and to following God's leading as He shows them how to love and serve one another a little better every day.

We've been through a lot, it seems. Many of our memories are wonderful, but those have been mixed with some really tough times. We've lived all of it together, sometimes seeing eye to eye from the outset; sometimes asking God to help us see it with the other's eyes. And knowing that building a marriage partnership is beyond us, we've always leaned on God for guidance.

Through all those experiences, we've hung on to two simple thoughts: first, that giving up on our marriage was never an option; and, second, we have to keep learning and applying biblical principles throughout the journey. We're not done learning. Some lessons came more easily than others. Some truths God is still unfolding for us.

Although we've told our story through the chronology of our three-decade-long marriage, we thought it might be interesting to examine our marriage in another way—by determining which biblical principles have continued to crop up in our life together. Therefore, in the appendix that follows, you'll find a list of "core principles" that we've pulled from the stories in this book. This is not meant to be an exhaustive list; God may have other biblical lessons for you that aren't on our list. These are the principles, though, that have guided us. Each is linked to a passage of Scripture that spoke to us, as well as to a relevant chapter of our story.

We pray that our list provides specific takeaways for your marriage. You might even use it as a springboard for discussion about some ways you and your spouse might draw closer together. Whether you're on rock solid footing with each other or the two of you are struggling to hold on, we pray that our story and our core principles encourage you to hang in there—together—while remembering that you don't need to do life alone. Never forget that the Lord walks beside you.

All the way.

Walk in Victory
Tony and Lauren Dungy

The Core Principles
of an Uncommon Marriage

Building a strong marriage requires more wisdom—not to mention grace—than any of us have in ourselves. That's why we believe that an uncommon marriage is built on biblical principles of love and unity, such as the ones we've listed below. If you want to trace any of these principles back to their source in the Bible, we encourage you to read the Scripture passages provided after each of the eight main points. If you want to look back to see how a specific practice played out in our marriage, we invite you to use the page numbers provided.

1. *Look to the Bible as your guidebook and to Christ as the living example for your marriage.*
   PSALM 1; EPHESIANS 5
   - Make Christ the center of your marriage (p. 160).
   - Treat your parents and others in authority with respect (pp. 10–11, 32).
   - Husbands: Work hard to hear your wife's heart and meet her needs (pp. 130–132).

- Husbands: Be prepared to love sacrificially (pp. 24–25, 130–133).
- Wives: Show love and respect to your husband (pp. 79–80, 84–87).
- Wives: Strike the right balance between acceptance and expressing your disappointment when following your husband's lead in an area where you disagree (pp. 79–80).
- Wait on God's timing; don't try to make things happen yourself (pp. 41–43, 84–87).
- Find your identity in Christ, not in the world (p. 109).
- Look to God as the source for all the stamina and patience you need (p. 160).
- Cling to each other and to God's promises that He is always with you when you face hard times (pp. 179–185).
- Prepare your mind and heart so you are ready for the opportunities God brings to you (pp. 81–87).
- Run to God rather than from Him when troubles come (pp. 145–150).

2. *Stay in sync spiritually.*
   PROVERBS 3:5-6; MATTHEW 18:19-20; ROMANS 8:26-30; JAMES 1:5
   - Communicate about spiritual matters—which should be the number one priority of your life (pp. 23–24, 81).
   - Look for opportunities to study the Bible with your spouse and/or in a small group (pp. 23–24).
   - Accept that the time and place where you connect spiritually as a couple may need to change along with the seasons of your marriage (pp. 23–24).

- Ask God to give you His infinite wisdom and to make you of one mind as you pray about decisions (pp. 24, 130–133).
- Remember that God will answer your prayers in His own timing—and in ways you might not expect (pp. 4–14, 93–96).
- Continue to pray together in the good times—that's often when couples make foolish mistakes (p. 103).
- Consider the input and wisdom of others when making decisions (pp. 42–43).
- Plug into a church that offers solid biblical preaching and where you feel at home (pp. 22–23, 78–79, 178–179).
- Seek out an older couple who can model a strong marriage and family life (p. 23).
- Be open to the possibility that the Lord is speaking to you through the input of your spouse (pp. 130–134).
- Share with each other the lessons you learn as you study the Bible (p. 81).
- Don't resist change when you see God bringing something new into your life (pp. 43–45).

3. *Manage Expectations and Appreciate Your Differences.*
   1 CORINTHIANS 12:14-21; EPHESIANS 4:2-7
   - Recognize that differing expectations are inevitable given different upbringings (pp. 10–12).
   - Be open to exploring new or different family traditions (pp. 11–12).
   - Don't expect your spouse to be able to read your mind (pp. 12–13, 68–71).

- Learn to adjust to and accept the "quirks" of your spouse's side of the family (pp. 31–32, 112–113).
- Train yourself to look for your spouse's strengths in his or her differences (pp. 135–137).
- Allow each spouse to take the lead in the area of his or her strength (p. 62).
- Seek outside counsel when expectations and differences are too great to work through on your own (p. 118).
- Be wise when picking your battles, understanding that your spouse probably doesn't intend his or her weaknesses to cause you grief (pp. 119–120).
- Recognize that God often brings together different types of people to complement each other and bring balance to a family (pp. 50–51, 132–138).
- Expect that you will see things differently at times (pp. 135–137).
- Engage in activities you both enjoy together, but allow each other to maintain separate interests as well (pp. 174–175).
- Model appreciation of differences by treating each of your children as an individual with distinct needs at school and interests at home (pp. 122–124, 197–198).

4. *Work as a Team.*

ECCLESIASTES 4:9-12; EPHESIANS 4:15-16

- Consciously think of your spouse as a valued teammate (pp. 103–110).
- Make a special effort to learn more about your spouse's passions and interests (pp. 12, 133–134, 204–209).

- Parent in a way that champions values, models character, and ensures each family member is doing what he or she needs to do that day (pp. 104–105).
- Seek coaching from trusted family members, friends, or counselors when you feel more like opponents than teammates (p. 118).
- Work to accomplish something important together; as you do, you'll see your marriage growing stronger (pp. 28–31, 110).
- Be intentional about noticing and addressing the needs of your spouse and children (pp. 82, 111–112, 133).
- Establish household routines to cut down on confusion and stress, but prioritize relationships over structure (pp. 59–60, 82, 111–113).
- Stay connected through date nights and joint activities (pp. 60–61, 82).
- Don't rush into making major decisions (pp. 130–133, 154–155).
- Consistently demonstrate support for your spouse (pp. 85–87, 180–181).
- Cherish every moment with family members (pp. 169–172).
- Treat your kids' sports and other activities as being just as important as anything else on your family calendar (pp. 111–112, 126, 191).

5. *Practice Committed Love.*
MATTHEW 19:4-8; I CORINTHIANS 13
- Commit to stay together, no matter what (pp. 14–15, 159–160).

- Spend time, if possible, getting to know each other before starting a family (p. 27).
- Be willing to sacrifice to support your spouse's passion (pp. 133–138).
- Be sensitive and considerate to your spouse during transitions (p. 84).
- Expect that life will bring some difficult times; don't let them pull you away from your spouse (pp. 179–185).
- Affirm and express love to your spouse—especially when he or she is going through tough times (pp. 84–87, 167–168).
- Be willing to step up and do a little more than usual when the situation requires it (pp. 103–110).
- Seek to keep your romance alive, but be aware that it's normal for feelings to fluctuate and change over time; don't let unrealistic expectations of constant romance diminish your commitment to—or satisfaction with—your relationship (pp. 159–160).
- Show the world that you are your partner's greatest fan (pp. 166–168, 194–195).
- Care for the needs of your spouse's family as an expression of your love for your husband or wife (pp. 146–147).
- Build an uncommon marriage by staying focused on each other and allowing God to lead you (pp. 216–218).
- Rest in the assurance that God, who promises never to leave or forsake you, knows what's ahead for your family (pp. 133–138, 149–150).

6. *Communicate Well and Often.*

PROVERBS 25:11; JAMES 3

- Learn as much as you can about each other and how you each communicate before you get married (pp. 5–13).
- Accept others' input when making decisions, but listen the most to God and to each other (pp. 42–43).
- Find a way to talk daily about what is happening in each other's life (pp. 60–62, 81–82).
- Listen to and value your spouse's intuition (pp. 145–146).
- Remember that complaining will always bring you down; gratitude will lift you up (pp. 79– 82).
- Model regular communication through family meetings (pp. 82, 111).
- Pay attention to and use your spouse's preferred form of communication (p. 110).
- Ask whether you both have peace and are on the same page before committing to a major decision (pp. 24, 130–133).
- Remember that, with your words, you are teaching your kids how to speak to others (pp. 142–143).
- Use technology to keep you connected; don't allow it to pull you apart (pp. 157, 161).
- Seek to honor your spouse and children by the way you speak about them to others (pp. 125–126).
- Remember that the way you are relating to each other is creating a blueprint for your kids (pp. 215–216).

7. *Don't Run Away from Conflict.*

PROVERBS 15:1; COLOSSIANS 3:13-15

- Watch what you say—even the truth can wound when

it's spoken in the wrong way or at the wrong time
(pp. 142–143).

- Avoid frustration and seek to understand each other's
  heart by praying together and talking with each other
  (pp. 24, 68–72).
- Practice thinking about an issue on which you disagree
  from your spouse's point of view (pp. 79–80, 84).
- Don't assume your spouse understands how you feel—
  particularly when life gets busy (pp. 68–71).
- Be bold and speak the truth in love (pp. 79–80).
- Expect that when your emotions and perceptions don't
  line up, conflict will occur (p. 83).
- Resolve conflict by trying to understand each other and
  talking about the best way forward (pp. 71–83).
- Defuse tension during a minor disagreement by apolo-
  gizing for your part (pp. 114–115).
- Maintain a positive attitude, even in tough times, by
  building friendships and finding activities you enjoy
  (pp. 77–89).
- Don't fear conflict; use it as a tool to understand each
  other better (pp. 113–115).
- Don't try resolving major disagreements when you're
  tired (p. 158).
- Allow each other to grieve differently, but be open to
  your spouse's need to talk (pp. 179–185).

8. Support Each Other in Serving Others.

PROVERBS 22:9; LUKE 12:48, 22:24-27

- Consider what gifts, position, and influence God

has given you as a platform to help other people
(pp. 106–108, 203–212).

- Discover joy by giving to others in a way that suits you both (pp. 116–118, 211–212).
- Use your resources and gifts in a way that glorifies God (pp. 27–31, 139–141).
- Be hospitable (pp. 62, 174).
- Model what a healthy marital relationship looks like to other young couples (p. 118).
- Don't spread yourself too thin; it's hard to serve well and joyfully when you're overcommitted (pp. 126–128).
- Remember that people are watching to see whether your actions and attitudes match your words (pp. 125–126).
- Be open to signals from your spouse that you are over-committed (pp. 157–158).
- Keep your priorities straight: put faith and family first (pp. 21, 112, 126).
- Consider what only you can do when deciding where to volunteer or what causes to support (pp. 128, 204).
- Focus on both partners' passions (pp. 133–134).
- Share the spotlight with your spouse whenever you receive credit or recognition (pp. 104–105, 194–195).

Acknowledgments

We would like to acknowledge our literary agent, D. J. Snell, for all his hard work on this project.

We would also like to thank Tyndale House Publishers, especially Kim Miller. They were a blessing to us from start to finish.

About the Authors

Tony Dungy is the #1 *New York Times* bestselling author of *Quiet Strength, Uncommon, The Mentor Leader,* and *The One Year Uncommon Life Daily Challenge.* He led the Indianapolis Colts to Super Bowl victory on February 4, 2007, the first such win for an African American head coach. Dungy established another NFL first by becoming the first head coach to lead his teams to the playoffs for ten consecutive years. He retired from coaching in 2009 and now serves as a studio analyst for NBC's *Football Night in America.* He is dedicated to mentoring others, especially young people, and encouraging them to live uncommon lives.

Lauren Dungy is an early childhood specialist and a *New York Times* bestselling children's book author. She serves as vice president of the Dungy Family Foundation, which helps meet the spiritual, social, and educational needs of those in her community. Lauren is also a national spokesperson for the iMom organization. She is involved in many charitable causes in the

Tampa area, which revolve around three central themes—Christian outreach, children, and education. The Dungys are the parents of nine children.

Nathan Whitaker holds degrees from Duke University, Harvard Law School, and the University of Florida, and has worked in football administration for the Jacksonville Jaguars and Tampa Bay Buccaneers. He has written six *New York Times* bestsellers and lives with his family in Florida.

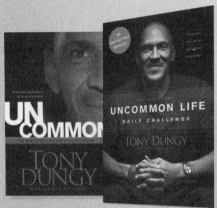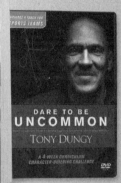

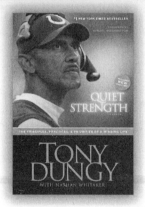
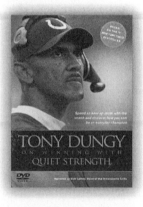
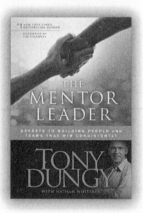

Tony and Lauren Dungy bring together their faith, love of children, and love of sports to tell stories of inspiration and encouragement.